Flash Kids
New York

MATH ADVENTURES

Grade 5

EDITED BY LINDA BERTOLA

ILLUSTRATIONS BY AGNESE BARUZZI

NOTE TO PARENTS

The mystery to learning math is to have fun!

This book series approaches math as an experience that should be playful, engaging, and relatable. Children will draw on their math and logic skills as they join the characters on an exciting adventure. This playful approach fosters a positive attitude about math and motivates children to keep trying and keep turning pages.

Research shows that children retain knowledge best when they take pleasure in learning. This book is designed to help children find pleasure in learning math skills.

This book offers a unique blend of math and mystery. As the adventure unfolds, each part of the story is a springboard for the activities in that section. With each new piece of the story, readers encounter new places and new math challenges. Readers gain confidence as they solve puzzles and problems on the road to completing the mission.

This book does not emphasize formal math definitions or terminology. Instead, math concepts are introduced gradually and naturally as the story unfolds. To reinforce concepts, suggestions for simple extension activities are included.

Children of different ages and math abilities can enjoy this book equally. They can engage with the material on many levels as they explore, reason, calculate, and have fun.

THIS BOOK IS
AIMED AT CHILDREN
IN GRADE 5.

Skills and Concepts Covered

- Adding, subtracting, multiplying, and dividing
- Comprehending equivalent fractions and ratios
- Comparing and adding fractions
- Solving logic puzzles
- Understanding patterns and number sequences

Tips for Adults

-Respect children's time and attention span.
If they close the book or skip a page, it does not mean they are giving up. Perhaps they just need to step away and revisit the material later.

-Ask questions instead of giving answers.
When children need help, pose questions to guide them to the problem or mistake.

-Let children set the pace, even if it seems slow or inefficient.
Later, you can always help them discover faster ways to solve a problem.

-Encourage children to think through problems before they begin solving.
Invite children to brainstorm by visualizing, discussing, drawing, or manipulating objects.

-Invite children to explain their process.
It is better for them to grasp the reasoning and logic behind a solution than to just memorize rules.

-Apply math to everyday life.
Help children discover numbers in the world around them. Point out how and when fractions are used for many daily activities.

THE MAGICAL MAGNIFYING GLASS

Tommy and Tina walk through the park on their usual route home from school. The afternoon sun shines on the path as Tina kicks at the pebbles. It's a typical Wednesday afternoon in the middle of a typical week.

Suddenly, a flash of light startles them. It's not the sun—it's something brighter, and it's moving! The light jumps from pebble to pebble and bounces off the path until it suddenly disappears.

"What was that?" Tina asks. They both look up and search the park for the mysterious light.

"I don't know, but there it is again!" Tommy points to the bright light as it glows from a patch of grass.

"Let's follow it," Tina shouts, grabbing Tommy's arm.

The light dances across the field, guiding the two friends to a small bush at the far edge of the park. Tina pushes the branches aside, and there, sitting among the dry leaves, is a magnifying glass.

"Someone must have tossed it into the bushes," Tina says.

"The sun probably reflected off of it and made that flash of light." Tommy reaches into the bushes to pick up the magnifying glass.

As soon as Tommy touches the handle, they hear a quiet voice. "Tommy and Tina, please listen to me. We need your help."

"Did you hear that?" Tina stares at the magnifying glass in shock. "Maybe we should just go home."

"It says it needs our help," Tommy points out. "I know this is wacky, but let's just listen."
Tina nods, and the two friends lean closer to the strange magnifying glass.

"I'll get right to the point," the Magnifying Glass says. "A secret agency sent me here to find you two. A villain named Mister X stole an ancient clay tablet. This tablet contains magic numbers. If we don't find it by midnight, all numbers will disappear from the world!"

"At least we wouldn't have any math homework," Tommy points out.

"That's true," Tina agrees, "but we also wouldn't have basketball or soccer games because we couldn't keep score. Without numbers to set the oven temperature, we couldn't bake cookies or cakes."

"Numbers are everywhere," the Magnifying Glass adds. "Home addresses, price tags, cars and planes, and of course phones!"

Tommy and Tina look at each other. They know they have to help.

"What can we do?" Tommy asked.

"The first step is to be trained for your mission," the Magnifying Glass explains. "Do you trust me?"

Tommy and Tina nod at the Magnifying Glass and stand up. "Let's go rescue the tablet, the numbers, and the world," Tina says.

FIRST, FIGURE OUT THE CODE NAME OF THE SECRET AGENCY. FIND THE CORRECT SPOT ON THE GRID, AND FILL IN EACH BOX ACCORDING TO THE KEY. A SPECIAL SYMBOL WILL BE REVEALED!

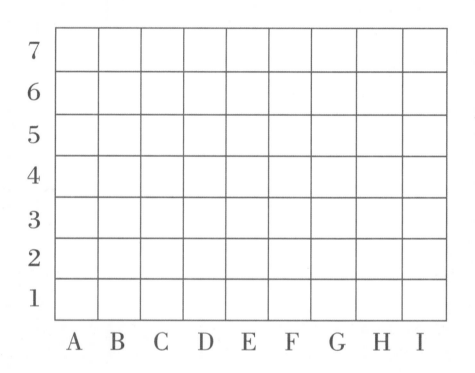

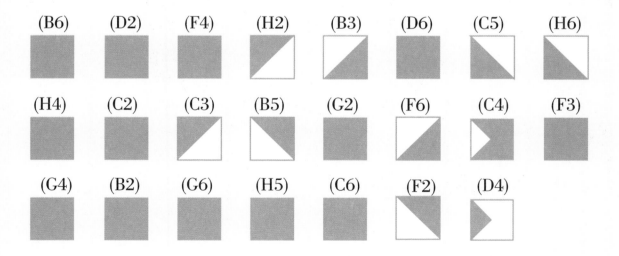

THE SYMBOL IS A GREEK LETTER CALLED A SIGMA. THE CODE NAME OF THE SECRET AGENCY IS SIGMA 2. TOMMY AND TINA MUST GO TO THE SIGMA 2 HEADQUARTERS. IT IS SURROUNDED BY TRAPS TO KEEP OUT SPIES.
THERE IS ONLY ONE WAY TO GET IN SAFELY. STEP ONLY ON STONES OR BOARDS WITH NUMBERS THAT ARE A MULTIPLES OF 4. IF THE NUMBER IS ALSO A MULTIPLE OF 6, DO NOT STEP ON IT!

SHOW THE CORRECT PATHS THAT TOMMY AND TINA MUST TAKE.

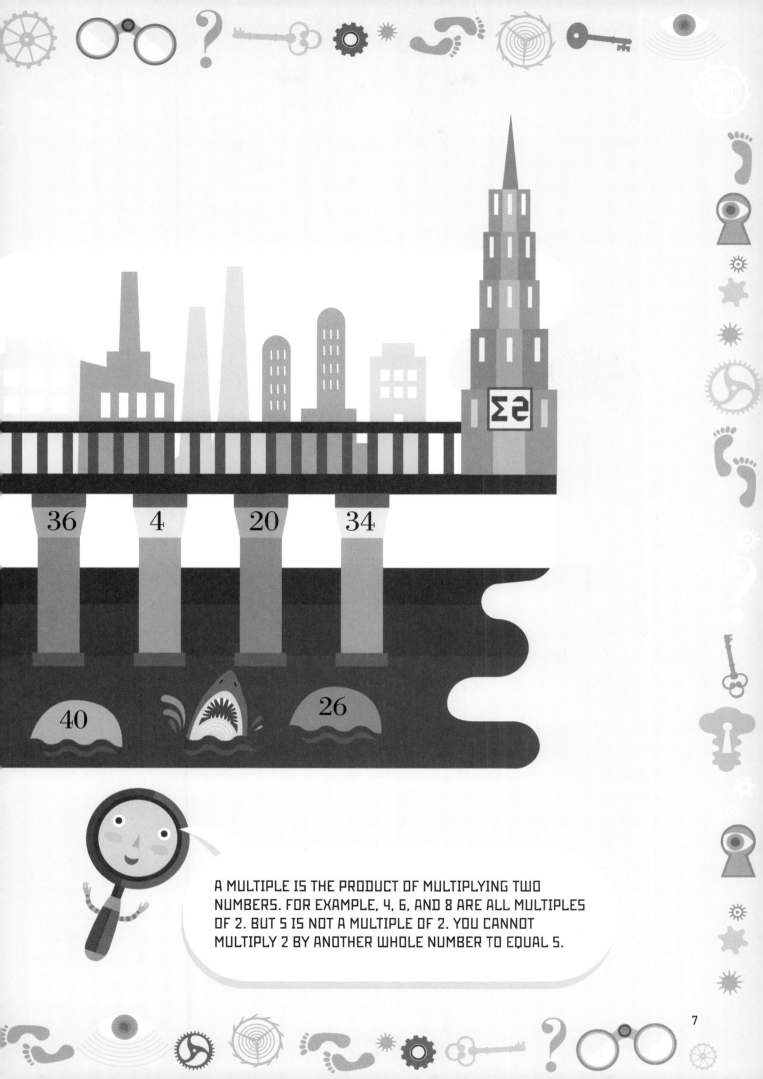

36 4 20 34

Σ2

40 26

A MULTIPLE IS THE PRODUCT OF MULTIPLYING TWO NUMBERS. FOR EXAMPLE, 4, 6, AND 8 ARE ALL MULTIPLES OF 2. BUT 5 IS NOT A MULTIPLE OF 2. YOU CANNOT MULTIPLY 2 BY ANOTHER WHOLE NUMBER TO EQUAL 5.

TOMMY AND TINA MADE IT INSIDE THE SIGMA 2 HEADQUARTERS. NOW THEY WILL BE TRAINED AS SECRET AGENTS. THEY MUST LEARN HOW TO STEP CAREFULLY AND AVOID TRAPS.

TOMMY MUST CROSS THE ROOM WITHOUT TRIGGERING THE ALARM. HE CAN ONLY STEP ON A TILE IF ITS NUMBER IS A MULTIPLE OF 7. FIND THE PATH OF TILES HE MUST FOLLOW TO CROSS SAFELY.

21   58   29   44
  26   61   35   16
70   148   49   91
  85   63   74   87
56   98   43   77
  53   39   42   13
7   210   14   24
  28   150   84   89
79   16   18   70

TINA MUST FOLLOW THE FOOTPRINTS. DIVIDE EACH NUMBER BY 3. IF THE ANSWER HAS A REMAINDER OF 2, COLOR THE FOOTPRINT. THEN TINA CAN STUDY THE COLORED FOOTPRINTS FOR CLUES.

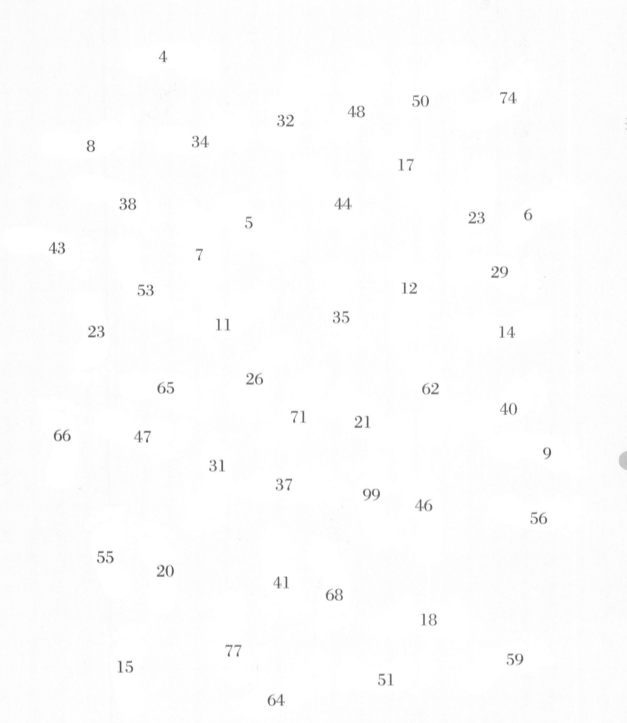

4

50   74

48

32

34   17

8

38   44   23   6

5

43

7

29

53   12

35   14

23   11

26   62

65   40

71   21

66   47   9

31

37   99

46

55   56

20

41

68

18

77   59

15

51

64

IT'S THE FINAL PHASE OF TRAINING. TOMMY AND TINA MUST LEARN HOW TO KNOW IF SOMEONE IS TELLING THE TRUTH.

HELP UNMASK THE LIARS. READ EACH STATEMENT. DO THE CALCULATIONS, AND WRITE TRUE OR FALSE BELOW EACH STATEMENT.

1) TWO EVEN NUMBERS CAN BE ADDED TOGETHER TO EQUAL AN ODD NUMBER.

2) HALF OF 48 IS EQUAL TO 12 DOUBLED.

3) THE DIFFERENCE BETWEEN THE SMALLEST FOUR-DIGIT NUMBER AND THE BIGGEST TWO-DIGIT NUMBER IS 901.

4) THREE TIMES 11 IS LESS THAN 12 TIMES 2.

5) IF YOU DOUBLE 8, FIND HALF OF THAT NUMBER, AND THEN DOUBLE IT, YOU GET 32.

6) SOME ODD NUMBERS ARE MULTIPLES OF 2.

7) 72 IS A MULTIPLE OF 3, 4 AND 6, BUT NOT 7.

8) THERE ARE NO NUMBERS WHICH ARE MULTIPLES OF BOTH 3 AND 2.

9) THE SUM OF TWO ODD NUMBERS IS ALWAYS EVEN.

10) IF A NUMBER IS A MULTIPLE OF 4, THEN IT HAS TO ALSO BE A MULTIPLE OF 2.

11) IF YOU TRIPLE 7 AND THEN DOUBLE THAT NUMBER, YOU GET 42.

MISSION TO THE WINDY TOWER

"Tommy and Tina, you have passed every test and completed your training," the Magnifying Glass announces proudly. "You are now officially Sigma 2 Secret Agents."

"What's our first mission?" Tina asks.

"It's complicated," the Magnifying Glass admits. "There are 15 pieces in the clay tablet, and you must gather them all."

"Fifteen pieces!" Tommy exclaims. "Where will we find them?"

"A trap door in the ground will take you to the Enchanted Forest. Once there, you must find the Windy Tower. This is where the first pieces of the tablet are."

Tommy and Tina look at the ground, and sure enough, a wooden door with a brass handle peeks out from the brush.

"So this trap door takes us to a magical forest?" Tommy asks, uncertainty creeping into his voice.

"Yes," the Magnifying Glass answers. "Every time you complete part of your mission, you'll find a trap door to take you to your next destination."

"I feel like I'm dreaming," Tina says.

"I know it seems strange," the Magnifying Glass says, "but there's no time to waste. You're on the trail of Mister X, and the fate of all numbers is in your hands. If you stay together and think smart, you can safely overcome any challenge. Good luck!"

Tommy and Tina open the trap door and peer into the dark passage. The two friends step to the edge of the opening, count to three, and then jump.

For a few moments, they tumble and flail in the darkness. But soon, their feet find the ground and they land with a thud. They stand up, dust themselves off, and take look around.

Miles of trees and green fields surround them. How will they ever find their way to the Windy Tower?

Tommy takes a few steps forward and stumbles. "Hey!" he says, scrambling to his feet. "This isn't just a tree root, it's the first clue!"

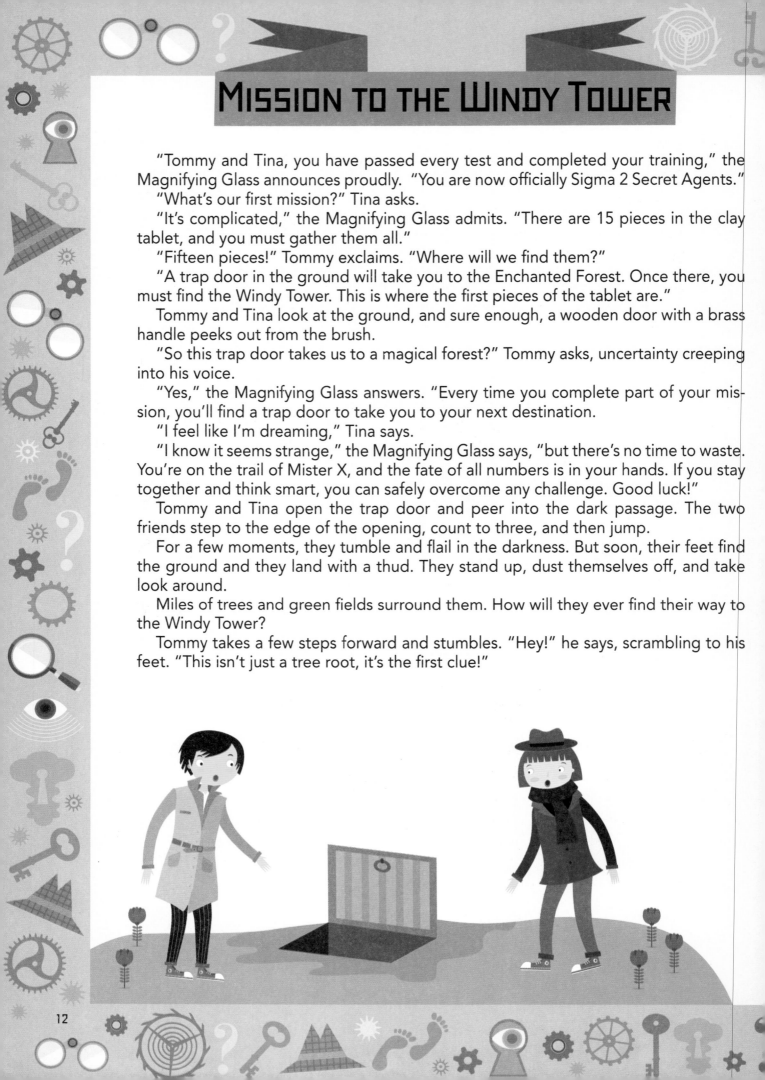

TOMMY AND TINA SEE 12 STICKS LAID ON THE GROUND IN THIS SHAPE.
THERE IS A NOTE NEXT TO THE STICKS:
"THESE STICKS NOW MAKE 5 SQUARES BIG AND SMALL.
TAKE AWAY 2 STICKS TO LEAVE 2 SQUARES IN ALL."
CROSS OUT THE STICKS TOMMY AND TINA SHOULD TAKE AWAY.

AS SOON AS TOMMY AND TINA SOLVE THE PUZZLE, THE NEARBY BRANCHES OPEN UP TO REVEAL A PATHWAY. AFTER THEY WALK A SHORT DISTANCE, THE PATH DIVIDES INTO FOUR. WHICH DIRECTION LEADS TO THE WINDY TOWER? THEY FIND THEIR NEXT CLUE IN THE MIDDLE OF THE CROSSROADS.

SOLVE THE PROBLEMS IN THE CLUES AND WRITE THE NUMBERS INTO THE PUZZLE. USE THE HIGHLIGHTED BOXES TO FILL IN THE MISSING NUMBERS ON THE COMPASS. TOMMY AND TINA SHOULD WALK IN THE DIRECTION THAT HAS THE HIGHEST NUMBER ON THE COMPASS.

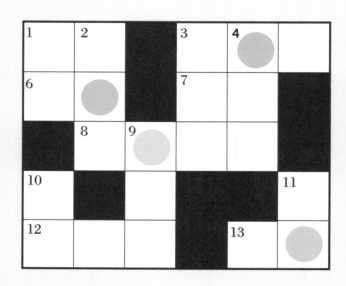

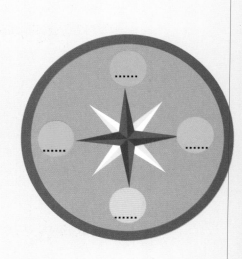

HORIZONTAL

1 4 TIMES 4 IS _____
3 THE NUMBER OF SECONDS IN 6 MINUTES _____
6 3 TIMES 8 _____
7 MULTIPLY THE NUMBER OF SEASONS IN A YEAR BY THE NUMBER OF SIDES ON A PENTAGON. _____
8 THE NUMBER THAT CONTAINS 1 TEN, 5 HUNDREDS, 8 THOUSANDS AND 5 ONES _____
12 A TENTH OF 1000 _____
13 DOUBLE THIS NUMBER TO GET 38 _____

VERTICAL

1 HALF OF 24 _____
2 4 TIMES 162 _____
3 THE HIGHEST NUMBER THAT YOU CAN MAKE WITH THE DIGITS 1, 2 AND 3 _____
4 ADD 5 TO 5 TIMES 120 _____
9 A QUARTER OF 2000 _____
10 A FIFTH OF 55 _____
11 THE LARGEST 2-DIGIT NUMBER _____

THE WIND WHIPS AGAINST TOMMY AND TINA AS THEY WALK EAST. BY THE TIME THEY REACH THE BOTTOM OF THE TOWER, THE WIND IS WILD AND FIERCE.

TOMMY AND TINA WANT TO GET INSIDE THE TOWER WHERE THE TABLET PIECES ARE HIDDEN. BUT FIRST, THEY MUST SOLVE ALL THE PUZZLES ON THE ANCIENT TOWER WALLS.

EACH LAYER OF THE WALL HAS A DIFFERENT NUMBER OF BRICKS. THE BRICKS IN EACH LAYER ARE EQUAL IN SIZE. WRITE THE CORRECT FRACTION ON EACH BRICK.

IN A FRACTION, THE TOP NUMBER IS CALLED THE **NUMERATOR**; THE BOTTOM NUMBER BOTTOM NUMBER IS CALLED THE **DENOMINATOR**. WHAT HAPPENS WHEN THE NUMERATOR STAYS THE SAME BUT THE DENOMINATOR GETS BIGGER? DOES THE VALUE OF THE FRACTION BECOME GREATER OR SMALLER?

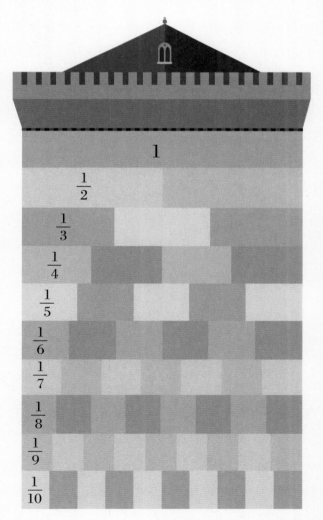

WRITE THE FRACTION FOR THE SHADED PART OF EACH WINDOW.

LOOK FOR WINDOWS WITH THE SAME FRACTION WRITTEN BELOW.
DO THEY HAVE THE SAME PATTERN TOO?

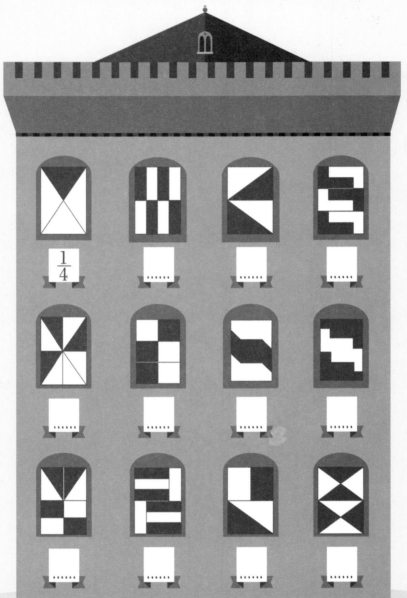

$\frac{1}{4}$

WELL DONE! YOU HAVE EARNED PIECE NUMBER 11 OF THE TABLET. FIND THE STICKER IN THE BACK OF THE BOOK AND PLACE IT ON PAGE 48.

DRAW LINES TO DIVIDE THE GRIDS INTO EQUAL PARTS ACCORDING TO
THE NUMBER AT THE TOP. THERE IS ONE RULE, THOUGH. EACH GRID
MUST LOOK DIFFERENT!

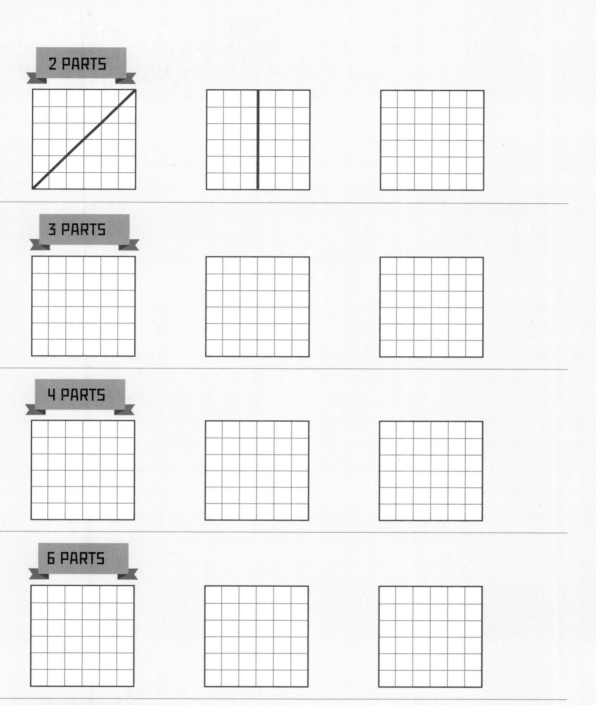

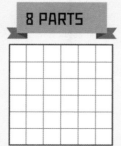
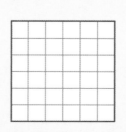
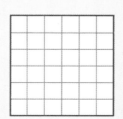

EACH SECTION OF GLASS IS A FRACTION OF THE WINDOW. COLOR EACH WINDOW SECTION ACCORDING TO THE KEY BELOW. BE CAREFUL! PIECES IN THE SAME WINDOW CAN HAVE DIFFERENT VALUES.

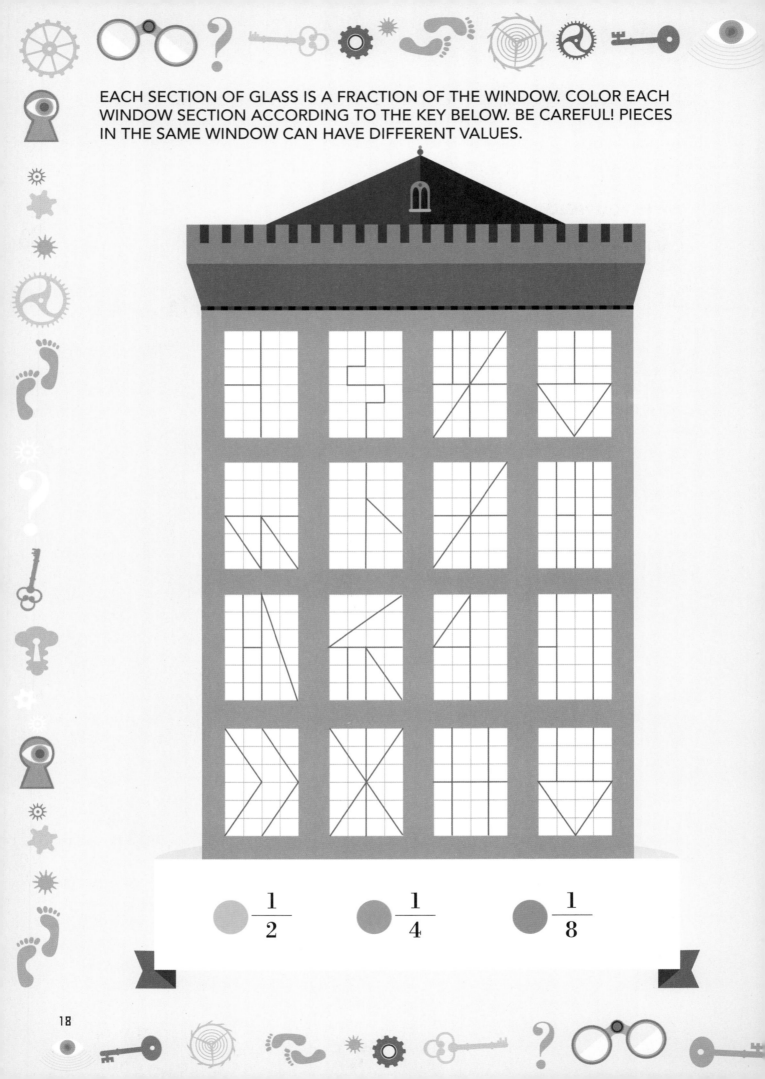

$$\frac{1}{2} \qquad \frac{1}{4} \qquad \frac{1}{8}$$

THE PUZZLES ARE SOLVED! THE DOOR OPENS WITH A CREAK, AND TOMMY AND TINA CAN ENTER THE WINDY TOWER.

MAKE YOUR OWN FRACTION WALL!

WHAT YOU NEED:
STICKERS FROM THE BACK OF THE BOOK
CARDBOARD
SCISSORS

DIRECTIONS:
1. PLACE THE STICKERS ON CARDBOARD.
2. CAREFULLY CUT ALONG THE LINES.
3. USE YOUR FRACTION WALL TO COMPARE FRACTIONS IN A FLASH!

WELL DONE! YOU HAVE EARNED PIECE NUMBER 2 OF THE TABLET. FIND THE STICKER IN THE BACK OF THE BOOK AND PLACE IT ON PAGE 48.

AS SOON AS TOMMY AND TINA STEP INSIDE, A CREATURE BLOCKS THEIR WAY.
"I AM STAG-HEAD!" HE BOOMS. "NOBODY HAS EVER SOLVED THE PUZZLES
TO ENTER MY TOWER. I SEE YOU'RE CLEVER . . . BUT NOT CLEVER ENOUGH TO
SOLVE MY NEXT PUZZLE!"

COMPARE THE FRACTIONS
IN EACH ROW. CIRCLE THE
SMALLEST NUMBER IN RED AND
THE LARGEST ONE IN BLUE.

$\frac{1}{5}$ $\frac{1}{8}$ $\frac{1}{2}$ $\frac{1}{3}$

$\frac{1}{6}$ $\frac{4}{6}$ $\frac{3}{6}$ $\frac{5}{6}$

$\frac{2}{8}$ $\frac{1}{5}$ $\frac{3}{7}$ $\frac{3}{6}$

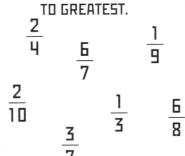

WRITE THESE FRACTIONS
IN A LINE FROM SMALLEST
TO GREATEST.

$\frac{2}{4}$ $\frac{6}{7}$ $\frac{1}{9}$

$\frac{2}{10}$ $\frac{1}{3}$ $\frac{6}{8}$

$\frac{3}{7}$

USE THE SYMBOLS <, >, OR = TO
COMPARE EACH SET OF FRACTIONS.

$\frac{1}{4}$ $\frac{1}{6}$ $\frac{5}{6}$ $\frac{4}{5}$

$\frac{4}{7}$ $\frac{2}{3}$ $\frac{1}{1}$ $\frac{9}{10}$

$\frac{4}{8}$ $\frac{1}{2}$ $\frac{2}{6}$ $\frac{1}{3}$

"WE WILL MAKE YOU A DEAL," TOMMY SAYS. "IF WE FAIL THE PUZZLE, WE WILL LEAVE. BUT IF WE SOLVE IT, YOU MUST GIVE US YOUR MEDALLION."

STAG-HEAD NODS, AND TOMMY WINKS AT TINA. INSIDE STAG-HEAD'S MEDALLION IS ANOTHER PIECE OF THE TABLET!

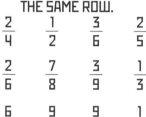

CIRCLE THE FRACTION IN EACH ROW THAT IS NOT EQUIVALENT TO THE OTHERS IN THE SAME ROW.

$\frac{2}{4}$ $\frac{1}{2}$ $\frac{3}{6}$ $\frac{2}{5}$

$\frac{2}{6}$ $\frac{7}{8}$ $\frac{3}{9}$ $\frac{1}{3}$

$\frac{6}{6}$ $\frac{9}{10}$ $\frac{9}{9}$ 1

WHAT FRACTION BELONGS IN THE EQUATION TO MAKE THE FINAL VALUE 1?

$\frac{4}{7}$ + ... = 1 $\frac{5}{10}$ + ... = 1

$\frac{1}{4}$ + $\frac{1}{2}$ + ... = 1   ...... + $\frac{2}{3}$ = 1

$\frac{2}{4}$ + $\frac{1}{8}$ + ... = 1

ADD THE FRACTIONS.

$\frac{1}{2}$ + $\frac{1}{2}$ = $\frac{1}{3}$ + $\frac{1}{3}$ =

$\frac{1}{2}$ + $\frac{1}{4}$ = $\frac{2}{3}$ + $\frac{1}{6}$ =

$\frac{4}{8}$ + $\frac{1}{2}$ = $\frac{3}{6}$ + $\frac{1}{4}$ + $\frac{2}{8}$ =

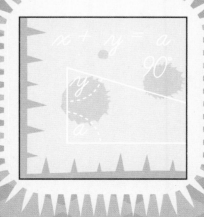

WELL DONE! YOU HAVE EARNED PIECE NUMBER 13 OF THE TABLET. FIND THE STICKER IN THE BACK OF THE BOOK AND PLACE IT ON PAGE 48.

The Adventure Heats Up

With the Stag-Head's tablet piece safely tucked away, Tommy and Tina know it's time to move on. But where is the next trapdoor?

They search the tower until Tommy calls out from behind a curtain. "I found it!"

Tina rushes to join him, and they quickly lift the door open. Taking care to protect all the tablet pieces, Tommy and Tina jump into the dark passage. They don't know where the portal leads, but they know more tablet pieces will be there.

They land more easily this time and stand up quickly to see where they are.

"I'm pretty sure the tablet pieces are hidden in there." Tommy points to a large castle in the distance.

Tommy and Tina begin walking toward the stately castle. Stone towers stretch toward the sky. Tall, thick walls and iron gates surround the castle. Getting in is not going to be easy. But Tommy and Tina are intrigued by the warmth coming from the castle. The closer they get, the more heat they feel.

Tommy and Tina pause at the castle gate, their eyes drawn to a flag covered in symbols.

"You're looking at my flag!" a voice booms from inside the castle. Tommy and Tina exchange worried glances, but they stand firm. "Those symbols come from the shields of all the knights who have tried to beat me. They all failed."

"Who or what is inside that castle?" Tommy whispers.

"I don't know, but we have to find out. Remember, the Magnifying Glass said if we stick together and think smart, we'll always be safe."

Tommy nods, stepping closer to the gate and the flag. "We're Sigma 2 Secret Agents. We can do it."

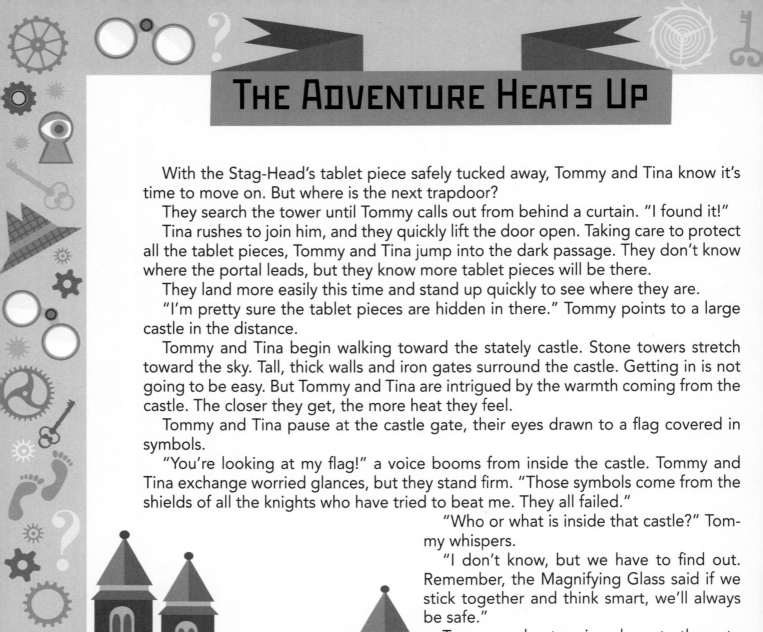

TO OPEN THE GATE, SHOW EACH FRACTION BY CORRECTLY SHADING PART
OF THE SHAPE NEXT TO IT.

HERE'S A TIP! COUNT THE TOTAL
SQUARES ON EACH SHAPE AND
DIVIDE THE SHAPE INTO PARTS WITH
AN EQUAL NUMBER OF SQUARES.

TOMMY AND TINA PASS THROUGH THE GATE AND FIND A SCALY, FIRE-BREATHING DRAGON GUARDING THE TABLET PIECE. THE DRAGON HAS SCORCHED AND BROKEN THE FLOOR TILES TO STOP THE CHILDREN FROM GETTING CLOSER.

RESTORE THE TILE PIECES SO TOMMY AND TINA CAN CROSS THE FLOOR. THE FRACTION SHOWS WHICH PART OF THE TILE IS FILLED IN. DRAW THE MISSING PART OF EACH TILE TO MAKE IT WHOLE AGAIN.

THE DRAGON HAS LEFT ANOTHER TRAIL OF TRICKY TILES. LOOK AT THE FRACTION FOR EACH ROW AND COLUMN. COLOR IN THE NUMBER OF SQUARES ACROSS OR DOWN TO REPRESENT THAT FRACTION.

HERE'S A TIP! LOOK FOR ROWS AND COLUMNS WHOSE FRACTIONS EQUAL 1. COLOR THE WHOLE ROW OR COLUMN FIRST. YOU CAN ALSO PUT A SMALL DOT IN BOXES THAT SHOULD STAY BLANK.

	$\frac{4}{4}$	$\frac{2}{4}$	$\frac{3}{4}$	$\frac{1}{4}$
$\frac{3}{4}$				
$\frac{1}{4}$				
$\frac{4}{4}$				
$\frac{2}{4}$				

	$\frac{1}{5}$	$\frac{3}{5}$	$\frac{5}{5}$	$\frac{3}{5}$	$\frac{1}{5}$
$\frac{1}{5}$					
$\frac{3}{5}$					
$\frac{5}{5}$					
$\frac{3}{5}$					
$\frac{1}{5}$					

	$\frac{5}{5}$	$\frac{2}{5}$	$\frac{3}{5}$	$\frac{1}{5}$	0
$\frac{4}{5}$					
$\frac{1}{5}$					
$\frac{1}{5}$					
$\frac{2}{5}$					
$\frac{3}{5}$					

	$\frac{5}{7}$	$\frac{7}{7}$	$\frac{3}{7}$	$\frac{6}{7}$	$\frac{3}{7}$	$\frac{6}{7}$	$\frac{3}{7}$
$\frac{7}{7}$							
$\frac{1}{7}$							
$\frac{4}{7}$							
$\frac{7}{7}$							
$\frac{3}{7}$							
$\frac{4}{7}$							
$\frac{7}{7}$							

WELL DONE! YOU HAVE EARNED PIECE NUMBER 8 OF THE TABLET. FIND THE STICKER IN THE BACK OF THE BOOK AND PLACE IT ON PAGE 48.

TAKE THE FRACTION CARDS FROM THE BACK OF THE BOOK AND GLUE THEM TO STURDY CARDBOARD. CUT THEM OUT AND USE THEM TO PLAY ONE OR MORE OF THESE GAMES!

GAME 1

FROM 2 TO 4 PLAYERS

HOW TO PLAY:
1. SHUFFLE AND DEAL OUT ALL THE CARDS TO PLAYERS. PLAYERS KEEP THEIR DECKS FACE DOWN IN FRONT OF THEM.
2. EACH PLAYER TAKES A TURN BY FLIPPING OVER THE TOP CARD AND PLACING IT FACE-UP IN THE MIDDLE.
3. IF THE FRACTION ON THE CARD HAS THE SAME VALUE AS THE PREVIOUS CARD PLAYED IN THE MIDDLE PILE, THE PLAYERS MUST SHOUT "SNAP!"
4. THE FIRST PLAYER TO PLACE THEIR HAND ON THE CENTER PILE WINS ALL THE CARDS IN THE PILE.
5. CONTINUE PLAYING UNTIL ONE PLAYER HOLDS ALL THE CARDS.

GAME 2

FROM 2 TO 4 PLAYERS

THIS IS A VARIATION ON GAME 1.
1. BEFORE BEGINNING, EACH PLAYER CHOOSES AN ANIMAL AND SHARES IT WITH THE OTHERS.
2. DEAL THE CARDS AND TAKE TURNS AS EXPLAINED IN GAME 1.
3. WHEN A CARD WITH AN EQUIVALENT FRACTION IS PLACED IN THE CENTER PILE, DO NOT PUT YOUR HAND ON THE PILE. INSTEAD, THE PLAYERS WHO PLACED THE TWO CARDS MUST MAKE THE SOUND OF THE OTHER PERSON'S ANIMAL. THE FIRST PERSON TO MAKE THE CORRECT SOUND TAKES ALL THE CARDS IN THE CENTER.
4. AS IN GAME 1, THE PLAYER WITH ALL THE CARDS AT THE END WINS THE GAME.

GAME 3

2 PLAYERS

1. DEAL OUT ALL THE CARDS BETWEEN THE TWO PLAYERS, KEEPING THE CARDS FACE DOWN IN FRONT OF EACH PLAYER.
2. BOTH PLAYERS FLIP OVER THE TOP CARD AT THE SAME TIME AND COMPARE.
3. THE PLAYER WHO HAS THE HIGHER FRACTION CARD WINS BOTH CARDS AND ADDS THEM TO HIS OR HER DECK.
4. IF THE CARDS SHOW EQUIVALENT FRACTIONS, BOTH PLAYERS PLACE ONE CARD FACE DOWN AND ANOTHER FACE UP. WHOEVER HAS THE HIGHER FRACTION NOW WINS ALL THE CARDS.
5. CONTINUE PLAY UNTIL ONE PLAYER HAS ALL THE CARDS.

COMPARE THE FRACTIONS INSIDE EACH CIRCLE OF FLAMES.
FOR SOME, YOU WILL NEED TO ADD TO GET THE TOTAL VALUE.
COLOR ALL FLAMES WITH EQUIVALENT VALUES THE SAME COLOR.

HERE'S A TIP! EQUIVALENT FRACTIONS HAVE THE SAME VALUE,
EVEN THOUGH THEY MIGHT LOOK DIFFERENT. FOR EXAMPLE,
$\frac{1}{2}$ IS THE SAME AS $\frac{2}{4}$ OR $\frac{3}{6}$. IN FACT, THERE ARE INFINITE
WAYS TO EXPRESS THE SAME FRACTION!

$\frac{4}{8}$

$\frac{3}{4}$

$\frac{1}{2} + \frac{2}{4}$

$\frac{2}{4}$

1

$\frac{1}{4}$

$\frac{2}{8}$

$\frac{1}{4} + \frac{4}{8}$

$\frac{1}{2} + \frac{1}{4}$

$\frac{6}{8}$

$\frac{1}{8} + \frac{1}{8}$

$\frac{1}{4} + \frac{2}{8}$

$\frac{1}{2} + \frac{1}{2}$

$\frac{1}{2}$

$\frac{6}{8} + \frac{2}{8}$

648 18
108 36
0

WELL DONE! YOU HAVE EARNED PIECE
NUMBER 5 OF THE TABLET. FIND THE
STICKER IN THE BACK OF THE BOOK
AND PLACE IT ON PAGE 48.

THE DRAGON LOVES CIDER! READ THE CLUES AND DRAW THE CORRECT AMOUNT OF CIDER IN EACH GLASS.

- THE FIRST GLASS IS $\frac{1}{2}$ FULL.
- THE SECOND GLASS CONTAINS HALF THE CIDER OF THE FIRST ONE.
- THE THIRD GLASS CONTAINS THE AMOUNT FROM THE FIRST AND SECOND GLASSES ADDED TOGETHER.

1) IF THE CIDER FROM ALL THREE GLASSES WAS POURED EQUALLY AMONG THE GLASSES, WHAT FRACTION OF EACH GLASS WOULD BE FULL?

_____

2) THE DRAGON HAS HIDDEN 25 MARBLES UNDER HIS FRONT PAWS. UNDER HIS RIGHT PAW THERE ARE 7 LESS THAN UNDER HIS LEFT PAW. EXACTLY HOW MANY MARBLES ARE UNDER EACH PAW?

_____

_____

THE DRAGON ALSO LOVES CHOCOLATE! HE EATS A LITTLE OF HIS CHOCOLATE BAR EVERY DAY. READ THE CLUES AND USE THE SQUARES ON THE BAR TO KEEP TRACK OF HOW MUCH HE EATS EACH DAY.

- ON MONDAY HE EATS HALF OF THE HALF OF THE BAR.
- ON TUESDAY HE EATS $\frac{1}{8}$ OF THE TOTAL.
- ON WEDNESDAY HE EATS HALF OF THE AMOUNT HE ATE ON MONDAY.
- ON THURSDAY HE EATS HALF OF WHAT AS MUCH AS HE ATE THE DAY BEFORE.
- ON FRIDAY HE EATS AS MUCH AS HE ATE ON TUESDAY AND WEDNESDAY COMBINED.
- ON SATURDAY HE EATS THE SAME AMOUNT AS HE DID HE DID ON THURSDAY.

3) HOW MANY CHOCOLATE SQUARES DOES THE DRAGON HAVE LEFT TO EAT ON SUNDAY? WHAT FRACTION OF THE WHOLE BAR IS SUNDAY'S PORTION?

_____

TOMMY AND TINA HAVE DISCOVERED THAT THEY CAN DISTRACT THE DRAGON WITH CHOCOLATE TO PUT OUT HIS FIERY FLAMES:

-THE DRAGON BREATHES A FLAME THAT IS 4 FEET LONG.

-EACH TIME HE EATS A CHOCOLATE, THE FLAME GETS SHORTER BY 1 FOOT.

-EACH TIME HE FINISHES THE CHOCOLATE, THE FLAME GROWS LONGER BY $\frac{1}{2}$ FOOT.

4) HOW MANY CHOCOLATES MUST TINA AND TOMMY GIVE THE DRAGON TO PUT OUT THE FLAME? (ONCE THE FLAME GOES DOWN TO 0 FEET, IT CANNOT GROW AGAIN!)

_____

_____

_____

5) AFTER EATING ALL THAT CHOCOLATE, THE DRAGON IS ALMOST READY TO GIVE UP THE TABLET PIECE . . . BUT ONLY IF TOMMY AND TINA CAN FIGURE OUT WHICH CHEST IT IS IN! THE SYMBOLS AND EQUATIONS ARE THE CLUES. WRITE THE FRACTION OF TOTAL JEWELS CONTAINED IN EACH CHEST. THE TABLET IS INSIDE THE CHEST WITH THE SMALLEST FRACTION.

■ + ■ = 1   ■ = ...

■ = ■ + ■   ■ = ...

■ = ■ + ■ + ■   ■ = ...

■ + ■ + ■ = ■   ■ = ...

WELL DONE! YOU HAVE EARNED PIECE NUMBER 1 OF THE TABLET. FIND THE STICKER IN THE BACK OF THE BOOK AND PLACE IT ON PAGE 48.

THE DRAGON LETS TOMMY AND TINA ENTER HIS GAME ROOM. IF THEY CAN COMPLETE THE PUZZLES AND PAINTINGS IN THE ROOM, THE DRAGON MIGHT GIVE THEM ONE MORE TABLET PIECE!

THE DRAGON HAS PAINTED $\frac{4}{6}$ OF THE PAINTING.
WHAT FRACTION OF THE PAINTING REMAINS TO BE COMPLETED?

_____

WHAT FRACTION OF THIS CHOCOLATE BAR HAS BEEN EATEN ALREADY? _____
WHAT FRACTION IS LEFT? _____

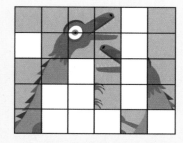

WHAT FRACTION OF THIS PUZZLE HAS THE DRAGON COMPLETED? _____
WHAT FRACTION MUST STILL BE COMPLETED? _____

THE DRAGON IS REPAINTING THIS OLD WARDROBE. HE HAS FINISHED _____ OF THE WARDROBE. HOW MUCH STILL NEEDS TO BE PAINTED?

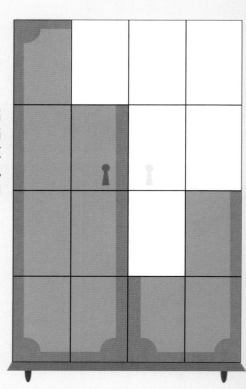

PARTS OF THIS IMPORTANT PAPER HAVE BEEN BURNED BY THE DRAGON. COMPLETE THE EQUATIONS SO THAT THE FRACTIONS ADD UP TO 1.

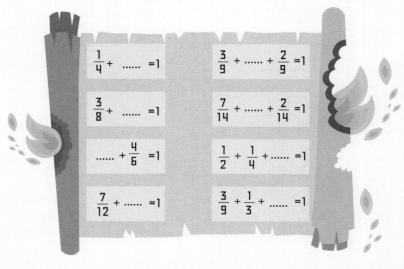

$\frac{1}{4} + \ldots = 1$

$\frac{3}{9} + \ldots + \frac{2}{9} = 1$

$\frac{3}{8} + \ldots = 1$

$\frac{7}{14} + \ldots + \frac{2}{14} = 1$

$\ldots + \frac{4}{6} = 1$

$\frac{1}{2} + \frac{1}{4} + \ldots = 1$

$\frac{7}{12} + \ldots = 1$

$\frac{3}{9} + \frac{1}{3} + \ldots = 1$

COLOR THE PIECES OF THIS PICTURE ACCORDING TO THE KEY BELOW.

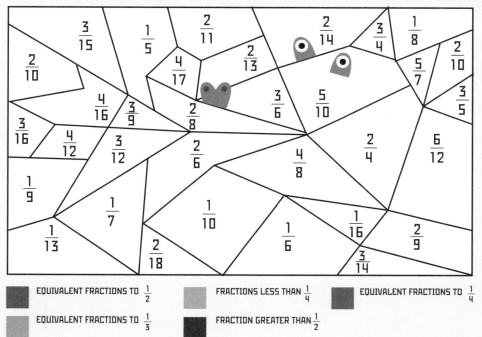

EQUIVALENT FRACTIONS TO $\frac{1}{2}$ FRACTIONS LESS THAN $\frac{1}{4}$ EQUIVALENT FRACTIONS TO $\frac{1}{4}$

EQUIVALENT FRACTIONS TO $\frac{1}{3}$ FRACTION GREATER THAN $\frac{1}{2}$

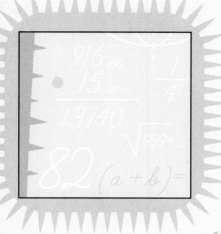

WELL DONE! YOU HAVE EARNED PIECE NUMBER 10 OF THE TABLET. FIND THE STICKER IN THE BACK OF THE BOOK AND PLACE IT ON PAGE 48.

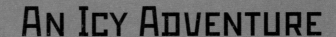

An Icy Adventure

Tommy and Tina are relieved they've defeated the dragon, but there's no time to rest. They search the room and find the next trap door on the closet floor. Holding tight to the four newest tablet pieces, they jump fearlessly into the portal. Gusts of cool air rush past them as they tumble down, a welcome change after the dragon's fiery flames.

This time, they make a soft landing on something powdery, white, and . . . cold.

"It's snow!" the two friends shout at the same time. Snow crunches under their feet as they stand up and look around. Miles of white snow and ice stretch out before them.

"Look over there," Tommy says, pointing across the icy field. Light glints off the ice. It looks like a small building could be out there, but it's difficult to see in the whiteness.

"Let's get closer and see what it is." Tina begins walking toward the glinting light, but she slips on the slick, icy ground. Tommy steadies her, and they catch the tablet pieces before they fall to the ground.

"That was close," Tommy says. "We need to find a safer way to get across the ice."

"How about those?" Tina says pointing to two planks of wood poking out from under the snow.

The children put the planks together and sit on them like a sled. Together, they push and slide across the ice until they reach the glinting building. It's a huge igloo! Tommy and Tina leave the sled and get closer to the entrance. There are three doors, and each one is guarded by a stern penguin.

"Only one door leads inside my ice castle," a voice echoes off the icy walls. "The other two doors lead straight to the dungeon. You only have one chance to get inside. You must solve a riddle."

Tommy and Tina glance at the tablet, noticing that more than half the pieces are still missing. More tablet pieces wait beyond the icy door. . . if only they can find the right one.

"We're ready," they say.

READ THE STATEMENTS AND FIGURE OUT WHICH PENGUINS
ARE LYING. THE PENGUIN WHO TELLS THE TRUTH GUARDS
THE CORRECT DOOR FOR TOMMY AND TINA.

1 OF US IS LYING

2 OF US ARE LYING

3 OF US ARE LYING

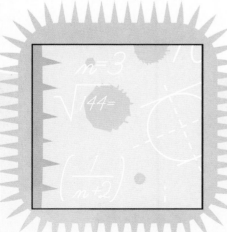

WELL DONE! YOU HAVE EARNED THE PIECE
NUMBER 4 OF THE TABLET. FIND THE
STICKER IN THE BACK OF THE BOOK
AND PLACE IT ON PAGE 48.

 BRRRRRRRRR. TOMMY AND TINA ARE INSIDE THE ICE CASTLE, BUT IT'S EVEN COLDER IN HERE THAN IT WAS OUTSIDE! THANKFULLY, THERE ARE SCARVES, SOCKS, AND HATS INSIDE. BUT THEY MUST EARN THESE WARM CLOTHES BY SOLVING THE PROBLEMS.

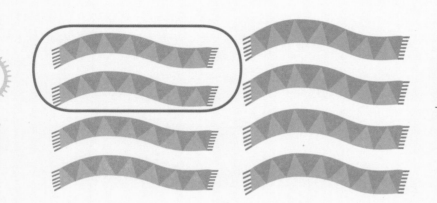

FIND $\frac{1}{4}$ OF 8 SCARVES

$\frac{1}{4}$ OF 8 = ($\frac{8}{4}$) X 1 = 2

FIND $\frac{3}{8}$ OF 16 SOCKS

$\frac{3}{8}$ OF 16 = (_____) X ____ = ____

FIND $\frac{2}{5}$ OF 15 HATS

$\frac{2}{5}$ OF 15 = (_____) X ____ = ____

$\frac{3}{7}$ OF 35 = _____

$\frac{5}{6}$ OF 42 = _____

$\frac{4}{9}$ OF 81 = _____

$\frac{2}{8}$ OF 24 = _____

TOMMY AND TINA ARE NOW TOASTY WARM AND READY TO RETRIEVE THE NEXT TABLET PIECE. BUT TO REACH IT, THEY MUST FIRST GET PAST ALL THESE SNOWMEN. COLOR IN THE HATS, SCARVES, AND GLOVES ACCORDING TO THE CLUES BELOW.

1) $\frac{1}{5}$ OF THE SNOWMEN HAVE RED GLOVES. _____

2) $\frac{3}{10}$ OF THE SNOWMEN WHO DO NOT HAVE RED GLOVES HAVE STRIPY SCARVES. _____

3) $\frac{4}{7}$ OF THE SNOWMEN LEFT HAVE A GREEN HATS. _____

4) HOW MANY SNOWMEN DO NOT HAVE RED GLOVES , GREEN HATS, OR STRIPED SCARVES?

_____

AS YOU WORK, TRY LABELING YOUR FRACTIONS TO HELP YOU REMEMBER WHAT THEY STAND FOR. IT COULD BE THE TOTAL, THE REMAINDER, OR SOMETHING ELSE.

WELL DONE! YOU HAVE EARNED PIECE NUMBER 7 OF THE TABLET. FIND THE STICKER IN THE BACK OF THE BOOK AND PLACE IT ON PAGE 48.

TOMMY AND TINA MADE IT PAST THE SNOWMEN AND INTO THE NEXT ROOM. THEY KNOW THE TABLET PIECE IS INSIDE THIS SPARKLING CHEST OF ICE. BUT THE BLUE LION GUARDS THE CHEST, AND IT HAS TWO LOCKS THAT MUST BE OPENED!

WRITE EACH PHRASE AS AN EQUATION AND SOLVE IT.
WRITE THE ANSWERS IN ORDER FROM SMALLEST TO LARGEST.
THIS IS THE COMBINATION TO OPEN THE FIRST LOCK.

1) DOUBLE 15 AND ADD 7. _____

2) SUBTRACT 5 FROM $\frac{4}{6}$ OF 48. _____

3) ADD $\frac{5}{8}$ OF 16 TO $\frac{7}{9}$ OF 36. _____

4) FIND $\frac{4}{5}$ OF 25. _____

5) MULTIPLY $\frac{3}{7}$ OF 21 BY $\frac{2}{8}$ OF 16. _____

6) FIND $\frac{2}{5}$ OF 125. _____

7) FIND 4 TIMES $\frac{4}{8}$ OF 56. _____

8) ADD HALF OF 18 TO $\frac{4}{7}$ OF 35 _____

☐ ☐ ☐ ☐ ☐ ☐ ☐ ☐

SOLVE THE PROBLEMS BELOW AND WRITE THE ANSWERS IN THE BOXES. THIS IS THE COMBINATION FOR THE SECOND LOCK.

1) $\frac{5}{7}$ OF THE CASTLE GUARDIANS WEAR RED GLOVES. IF THERE ARE 63 GUARDIANS IN TOTAL, HOW MANY OF THEM WEAR RED GLOVES? _____

2) THERE ARE 56 DOORS IN THE CASTLE, AND $\frac{5}{8}$ OF THEM ARE MADE OF OAK WOOD. HOW MANY DOORS ARE NOT MADE OF OAK WOOD?
_____

3) THE BLUE LION HAS 54 GOLD COINS. EVERY DAY HE SPENDS $\frac{1}{9}$ OF THE INITIAL AMOUNT. AT THE END OF THE WEEK, HOW MUCH MONEY DOES HE HAVE LEFT? _____

4) IN THE ICE CASTLE, TIME PASSES AT A DIFFERENT PACE. IN FACT, ONE MINUTE IN THE ICE CASTLE EQUALS $\frac{3}{4}$ OF A MINUTE IN THE REAL WORLD. SO, 5 MINUTES IN THE REAL WORLD EQUALS HOW MANY SECONDS IN THE ICE CASTLE?
_____

WELL DONE! YOU HAVE EARNED PIECE NUMBER 12 OF THE TABLET. FIND THE STICKER IN THE BACK OF THE BOOK AND PLACE IT ON PAGE 48.

1) THE BLUE LION HAS 840 GEMSTONES.
$\frac{3}{5}$ ARE RUBIES AND THE OTHERS ARE SAPPHIRES. HOW MANY RUBIES
AND HOW MANY SAPPHIRES DOES HE HAVE?

_____

_____

2) THE LION EXCHANGES $\frac{3}{14}$ OF HIS GEMS FOR A RARE
AND VALUABLE DIAMOND.
HOW MANY GEMS DOES HE HAVE AFTER THE EXCHANGE?

_____

_____

3) THERE ARE A TOTAL OF 36 GUARDIANS OF THE ICE CASTLE,
INCLUDING WALRUSES, SEALS, AND PENGUINS. THE PENGUINS MAKE
UP $\frac{3}{6}$ OF THE TOTAL. THERE ARE 4 MORE WALRUSES THAN SEALS.
HOW MANY OF EACH ANIMAL ARE THERE?

_____

_____

4) THE BLUE LION HAS COLLECTED 125 ANCIENT BOOKS FOR HIS LIBRARY. $\frac{2}{5}$ OF THE BOOKS ARE ABOUT GLACIERS. OF THE REMAINING BOOKS, $\frac{2}{3}$ ARE ABOUT SNOWSTORMS. THE REST OF THE BOOKS ARE ABOUT IGLOOS. HOW MANY BOOKS ARE THERE ON EACH SUBJECT?

_____

_____

5) THE BLUE LION'S FAVORITE DRINK IS ELDERBERRY JUICE. ONE BOTTLE CONTAINS $\frac{3}{4}$ OF A LITER OF JUICE. IF THE BLUE LION HAS 16 BOTTLES, HOW MANY LITERS DOES HE HAVE IN ALL? IF HE DRINKS HALF A LITER OF ELDERBERRY JUICE EVERY DAY, HOW LONG WILL THE 16 BOTTLES LAST?

_____

_____

WELL DONE! YOU HAVE EARNED PIECE NUMBER 3 OF THE TABLET. FIND THE STICKER IN THE BACK OF THE BOOK AND PLACE IT ON PAGE 48.

THE FINAL PIECES

Minutes pass as Tommy and Tina search the Blue Lion's icy lair for the next trap door.

"What time is it?" Tommy asks. "We need to find all the pieces before midnight, right?"

"Oh no!" Tina cries, looking at her watch. "I can hardly see the numbers on my watch."

"Numbers are starting to disappear from the world," Tommy says. "We have to hurry!"

"I found it!" Tina pries open the heavy trap door.

"We've been through wind, fire, and ice. What more could be in store for us?" Tommy peers into the darkness.

"There's only one way to find out." Tina tucks the tablet safely under her arm. "Jump!"

The journey feels longer this time, and the cold air of the ice castle quickly fades behind them. The tablet is heavier now that so many pieces have been filled in. Thankfully, they land in something soft and warm.

"It's sand!" Tommy says, struggling to his feet. He looks out across miles of golden sand dunes.

"Look!" Tina says. "Are those pyramids?" She points toward the tips of triangular buildings in the distance.

"There's only one way to find out." Tommy winks at her, and they set off across the deep sand.

They quickly shed their scarves and gloves as they trudge across the hot desert. They know every second counts. Soon, they stand at the base of a huge, majestic pyramid. Tommy and Tina know that the final four tablet pieces lay somewhere inside. They must find a way, and they must do it quickly.

MISTER X IS INSIDE THE PYRAMID WITH THE FINAL PIECES OF THE TABLET!
BUT TOMMY AND TINA MUST SOLVE A TRICKY PUZZLE TO GET INSIDE.
THERE ARE NINE BRICKS ARRANGED IN A SQUARE. DRAW FOUR LINES
TO CONNECT ALL THE BRICKS. YOUR PENCIL MUST ALWAYS TOUCH
THE PAPER!

HERE'S A TIP! TRY THINKING OUTSIDE THE BOX.

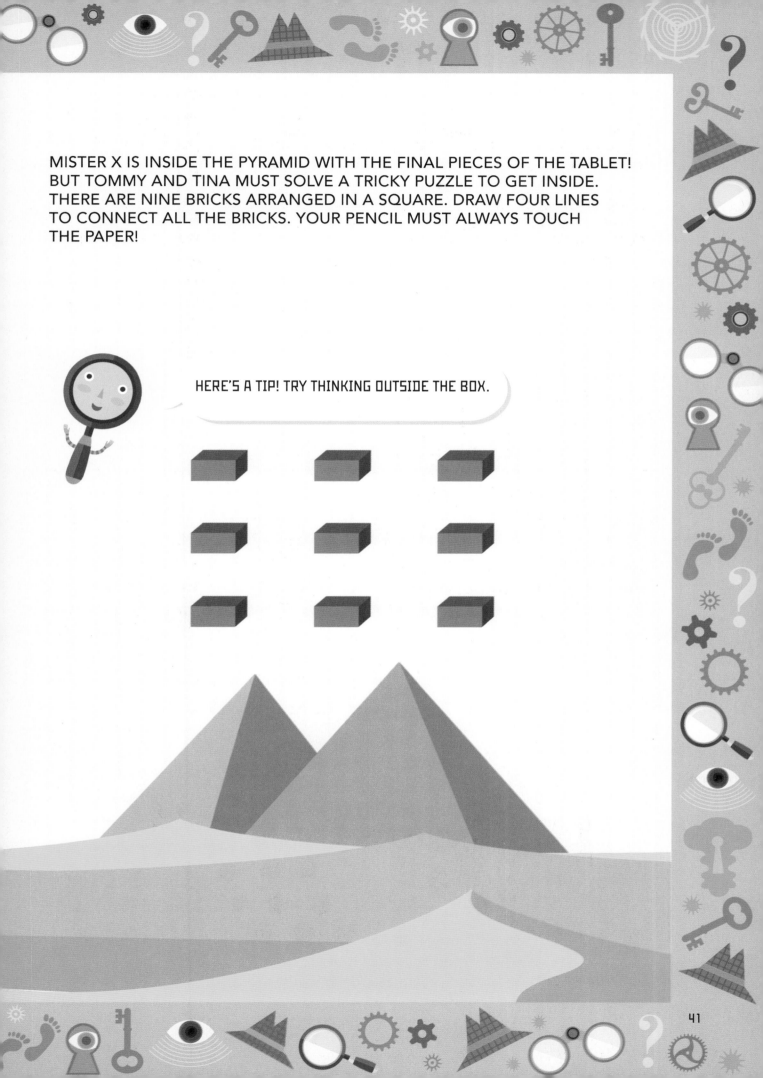

TOMMY AND TINA ARE INSIDE THE PYRAMID! THEY SEE A TABLE WITH 4 GROUPS OF ITEMS. TO GO ANY FURTHER, THEY MUST FIRST SOLVE THESE PUZZLES.

FOR EACH GROUP, SOME OF THE ITEMS ARE LAYING OUT, AND SOME ARE HIDDEN UNDER A GLASS. THE FRACTIONS SHOW HOW MANY ITEMS ARE VISIBLE ON THE TABLE. FIGURE OUT THE NUMBER OF ITEMS HIDDEN UNDER EACH GLASS AS WELL AS THE TOTAL NUMBER OF EACH ITEM.

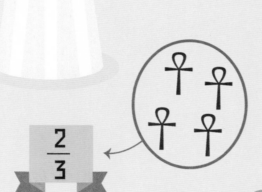

$\frac{2}{3}$ OF THE AMULETS ARE ON THE TABLE. HOW MANY ARE HIDDEN UNDER THE GLASS?

_____

HOW MANY AMULETS ARE THERE IN TOTAL?

_____

HOW MANY COINS ARE HIDDEN UNDER THE GLASS?

_____

HOW MANY COINS ARE THERE IN TOTAL?

_____

HOW MANY BEETLES ARE HIDDEN UNDER THE GLASS?

_____

HOW MANY BEETLES ARE THERE IN TOTAL?

_____

HOW MANY RED PENDANTS ARE HIDDEN UNDER THE GLASS?

_____

HOW MANY PENDANTS ARE THERE IN TOTAL?

_____

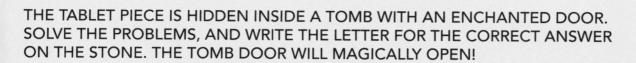

THE TABLET PIECE IS HIDDEN INSIDE A TOMB WITH AN ENCHANTED DOOR. SOLVE THE PROBLEMS, AND WRITE THE LETTER FOR THE CORRECT ANSWER ON THE STONE. THE TOMB DOOR WILL MAGICALLY OPEN!

1) THERE ARE MUMMIES IN THE GOLDEN TOMB AND IN THE STONE TOMB. THE GOLDEN TOMB CONTAINS 16 MUMMIES, WHICH IS $\frac{8}{15}$ OF THE TOTAL MUMMIES IN THE PYRAMID. HOW MANY MUMMIES ARE THERE TOTAL IN THE PYRAMID?
A) 28   B) 30   C) 14

2) THE SCRIBE HAS DRAWN 120 HIEROGLYPHS, WHICH IS 8/13 OF $\frac{8}{13}$ HIS TOTAL WORK. HE SPENDS 5 MINUTES DRAWING EACH HIEROGLYPH. HOW MUCH LONGER WILL IT TAKE HIM TO FINISH DRAWING THE REST OF THE HIEROGLYPHS?
A) 265   B) 195   C) 375

3) THE PHARAOH'S TREASURE HAS RUBIES, EMERALDS, AND SAPPHIRES. THERE ARE 60 SAPPHIRES, WHICH MAKE UP $\frac{4}{7}$ OF THE TOTAL TREASURE. THERE ARE 5 MORE RUBIES THAN EMERALDS. HOW MANY EMERALDS ARE IN THE PHARAOH'S TREASURE?
A) 40   B) 20   C) 25

WRITE THE LETTER FOR THE CORRECT
ANSWER ON EACH STONE.

WELL DONE! YOU HAVE EARNED PIECE NUMBER 9 OF THE TABLET. FIND THE STICKER IN THE BACK OF THE BOOK AND PLACE IT ON PAGE 48.

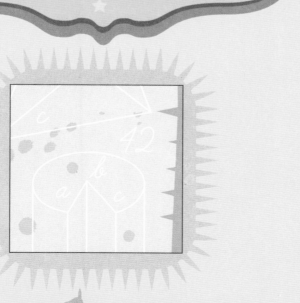

IT'S GETTING CLOSE TO MIDNIGHT! THANKFULLY, TOMMY AND TINA ARE FINALLY INSIDE THE TOMB. ANCIENT ITEMS FILL THE TOMB AND PICTURES COVER THE WALLS. THE TABLET PIECE WILL BE REVEALED WHEN ALL THE QUESTIONS ABOUT THE TOMB ARE ANSWERED. WORK CAREFULLY, BUT QUICKLY!

FIGURE OUT THE AGES OF THE PHARAOH'S THREE CHILDREN IN THIS PICTURE. THE PHARAOH WAS 36. THE SUM OF HIS CHILDREN'S AGES WAS DOUBLE $\frac{1}{6}$ OF THEIR FATHER'S AGE. THE OLDEST CHILD WAS DOUBLE THE AGE OF THE TWINS. WRITE THE CORRECT AGE ABOVE EACH PICTURE.

_____

_____

_____

2 INCHES

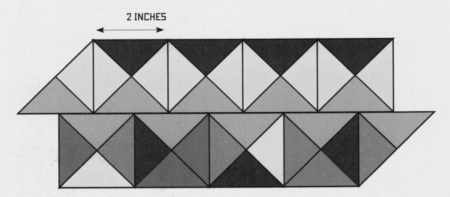

A SPECIAL TRIANGULAR DESIGN COVERS THE TOMB WALLS. THE LONGEST EDGE OF EACH TRIANGLE IS 2 INCHES. FIND THE FOLLOWING MEASUREMENTS:
1) TOTAL SURFACE AREA OF THE DECORATION: _____
2) SURFACE AREA OF THE ORANGE PIECES: _____
3) SURFACE AREA OF THE GREEN PIECES: _____
4) SURFACE AREA OF THE LIGHT BROWN PIECES: _____
5) SURFACE AREA OF THE DARK BROWN PIECES: _____
6) SURFACE AREA OF THE YELLOW PIECES: _____

100 GEMS ARE DIVIDED INTO 4 CHESTS. THE THIRD CHEST CONTAINS HALF OF THE TOTAL GEMS. THE FIRST CHEST CONTAINS $\frac{3}{5}$ OF THE REMAINING GEMS. THE SECOND CHEST CONTAINS $\frac{2}{3}$ OF THE GEMS INSIDE THE FOURTH CHEST. BELOW EACH CHEST, WRITE THE NUMBER OF GEMS IT CONTAINS.

_____

THE PHARAOH'S POETRY IS WRITTEN ON THESE ANCIENT PARCHMENTS. THE TOMB HAS MORE THAN 5 PARCHMENTS, BUT LESS THAN 40. THE PARCHMENTS CAN BE DIVIDED INTO 5 EQUAL GROUPS. IF YOU DIVIDE THE PARCHMENTS INTO GROUPS OF 4, THERE IS 1 LEFT OVER. HOW MANY TOTAL PARCHMENTS ARE IN THE TOMB?

_____

IN ANCIENT EGYPT, BEETLES WERE A SIGN OF GOOD LUCK. $\frac{2}{3}$ OF ALL THE BEETLES ON THE WALL ARE GOLD. $\frac{1}{2}$ OF ALL THE BEETLES ON THE WALL HAVE GEMS ON THEIR BACKS. HOW MANY GOLDEN BEETLES DEFINITELY HAVE GEMS ON THEIR BACKS?

....

....

WELL DONE! YOU HAVE EARNED PIECE NUMBER 6 OF THE TABLET. FIND THE STICKER IN THE BACK OF THE BOOK AND PLACE IT ON PAGE 48.

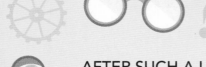
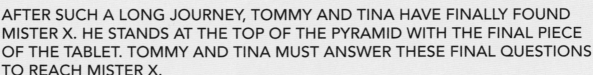

AFTER SUCH A LONG JOURNEY, TOMMY AND TINA HAVE FINALLY FOUND MISTER X. HE STANDS AT THE TOP OF THE PYRAMID WITH THE FINAL PIECE OF THE TABLET. TOMMY AND TINA MUST ANSWER THESE FINAL QUESTIONS TO REACH MISTER X.

THE AGE OF THE MUMMIES

1) ADDING THE AGES OF THE THREE MUMMIES TOGETHER TOTALS 624 YEARS. TWO MUMMIES ARE THE SAME AGE. THE THIRD IS TWICE THEIR AGE. HOW OLD IS EACH MUMMY?

_____

_____

THE TANK OF THE CROCODILES

2) START WITH A MYSTERY NUMBER. SUBTRACT 2 HUNDREDS. ADD 4 TENS. NOW DIVIDE IT IN HALF, AND YOU GET 144. WHAT IS THE MYSTERY NUMBER YOU STARTED WITH? _____

_____

START WITH A MYSTERY NUMBER. TAKE $\frac{5}{8}$ OF THAT NUMBER AND DOUBLE IT. NOW YOU HAVE 90. WHAT IS THE MYSTERY NUMBER YOU STARTED WITH? _____

_____

START WITH A MYSTERY NUMBER. ADD 2 TENS. IF YOU TAKE $\frac{2}{7}$ 7 OF THAT NUMBER, YOU GET 24. WHAT IS THE MYSTERY NUMBER YOU STARTED WITH? _____

_____

_____

THE TOMBS

3) WHO DOES EACH TOMB BELONG TO?

TAMES IS TO THE RIGHT OF AMES, BUT TO THE LEFT OF LAMES

RAMES RESTS IN THE CENTRAL TOMB

NAMES RESTS NEXT TO AMES

NAMES IS NOT IN THE FIFTH TOMB TO THE LEFT

TAMES IS BETWEEN RAMES AND LAMES

THE BRICKS

4) 1 BRICK WEIGHS 3 POUNDS MORE THAN HALF A BRICK. HOW MUCH DO 5 BRICKS WEIGH?

_____

_____

THE TANGLED BANDAGES

5) MISTER X LEFT A TANGLED BANDAGE IN THE CHILDREN'S PATH. THE BANDAGE IS 63 FEET LONG. TOMMY AND TINA CAN ROLL UP 6 FEET IN ONE MINUTE. BUT THE WIND ALSO UNROLLS 3 FEET EVERY MINUTE. HOW MANY MINUTES WILL IT TAKE TOMMY AND TINA TO ROLL UP THE WHOLE BANDAGE?

_____

_____

MISTER X

6) TOMMY AND TINA ARE SO CLOSE, BUT TIME IS ALMOST OUT. THIS HOURGLASS CONTAINS THE FINAL PUZZLE!
THE HOURGLASS HAD 1 MINUTE OF TIME LEFT. BUT MISTER X REMOVED 2/6 OF THE GRAINS OF SAND. HALF OF THE REMAINING SAND HAS ALREADY FALLEN. HOW MANY SECONDS ARE LEFT BEFORE MIDNIGHT?

_____

_____

_____

WELL DONE!
YOU HAVE EARNED PIECES NUMBER 14-15 OF THE TABLET.
LOOK FOR THEM AMONG THE STICKERS AND STICK THEM ON PAGE 48

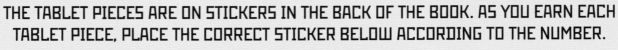

THE TABLET PIECES ARE ON STICKERS IN THE BACK OF THE BOOK. AS YOU EARN EACH TABLET PIECE, PLACE THE CORRECT STICKER BELOW ACCORDING TO THE NUMBER.

1	2	3
4	5	6
7	8	9
10	11	12
13	14	15

WELL DONE!

AS A SIGMA 2 SECRET AGENT,
YOU HAVE RESTORED THE
ANCIENT TABLET AND PROTECTED
ITS MAGICAL NUMBERS!

AS SOON AS TOMMY AND TINA FIT THE FINAL PIECE INTO THE TABLET, A FLASH OF LIGHT SURROUNDS THEM. THE NUMBERS LIFT FROM THE CLAY TABLET AND FLOAT OUT INTO THE WORLD. NUMBERS THAT HAD VANISHED FROM THERMOMETERS, SIGNS, AND COINS SUDDENLY REAPPEAR. PHONES BEGIN TO RING AND CHIME AS THEIR KEYPADS GLOW AGAIN. CROWDS CHEER AS SCOREBOARDS LIGHT UP TO SHOW THE WINNING TEAM. NUMBER AFTER NUMBER FINDS ITS PLACE AS EVERYTHING RETURNS TO NORMAL.

AS THE LIGHT FADES, TOMMY AND TINA SUDDENLY FIND THEMSELVES BACK AT THE PARK, EXACTLY WHERE THEY STARTED.

"WE DID IT!" TINA CHEERS. SHE CHECKS THE NUMBERS ON HER WATCH AND SMILES.

"THERE'S STILL ONE PROBLEM THOUGH," TOMMY ADMITS. "THE PAGES IN OUR MATH BOOK AREN'T BLANK ANYMORE. SO NOW WE HAVE TO DO OUR MATH HOMEWORK FOR TOMORROW!"

TINA LAUGHS. "AFTER ALL THIS PRACTICE, WE'LL FINISH OUR HOMEWORK IN A FLASH."

"A FLASH?" TOMMY SEARCHES THE PARK, REMEMBERING THE FLASH OF LIGHT THAT STARTED THEIR ADVENTURE.

"DON'T WORRY, WE'RE SIGMA 2 SECRET AGENTS NOW," TINA SAYS. "WE CAN HANDLE ANYTHING THAT COMES OUR WAY."

"EVEN HOMEWORK." TOMMY WINKS, AND THE TWO FRIENDS START TOWARD HOME.

ANSWERS

BANNERS MARKED WITH AN * SHOW JUST ONE OF MANY POSSIBLE CORRECT ANSWERS FOR THE PROBLEMS ON THAT PAGE.

P. 5: THE CODE NAME OF THE AGENCY

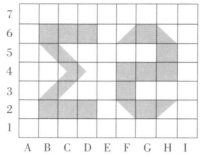

PP. 6-7: THE PATHS TO THE HEADQUARTERS

NUMBERS THAT ARE MULTIPLES OF 4 BUT NOT OF 6 ARE: 4, 8, 16, 20, 28, 32, 40, 44
TINA STEPS ON THE NUMBERS 44, 32, 4, AND 20.
TOMMY STEPS ON 28, 16, 8, AND 40.

P. 9: FOLLOW THE FOOTPRINTS

P. 8: FIND THE PATH ACROSS THE TILES

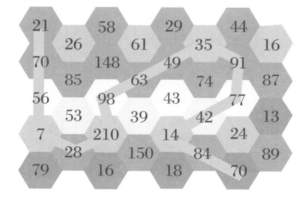

PP. 10-11: FINAL TRAINING LESSON

1. **FALSE** TWO EVEN NUMBERS WILL ALWAYS ADD UP TO AN EVEN NUMBER.
2. **TRUE** 48 HALVED EQUALS 24, AND 12 DOUBLED ALSO EQUALS 24.
3. **TRUE** THE SMALLEST FOUR-DIGIT NUMBER IS 1000, AND THE BIGGEST TWO-DIGIT NUMBER IN 99. IF YOU CALCULATE 1000-99 YOU GET 901.
4. **FALSE** THREE TIMES 11 EQUALS 33, AND 12 TIMES 2 EQUALS 24. 33 IS NOT LESS THAN 24.
5. **FALSE** IF YOU DOUBLE 8 YOU GET 16. HALF OF 16 IS 8, SO IF YOU DOUBLE THAT YOU GET 16 AGAIN.
6. **FALSE** ODD NUMBERS CANNOT BE MULTIPLES OF 2.
7. **TRUE** 72 IS A MULTIPLE OF 3, 4, AND 6, BUT 7 DOES NOT DIVIDE EVENLY INTO 72.
8. **FALSE** 6, 12, 18, 24, AND MANY OTHER NUMBERS ARE MULTIPLES OF BOTH 3 AND 2.
9. **TRUE** THE SUM OF TWO ODD NUMBERS IS ALWAYS EVEN. FOR EXAMPLE, 13 + 13 = 26.
10. **TRUE** 4 IS A MULTIPLE OF 2. SO, IF A NUMBER IS A MULTIPLE OF 4, IT IS ALSO A MULTIPLE OF 2.
11. **TRUE** 7 X 3 = 21. THE DOUBLE OF 21 IS 42.

P. 13: REMOVE 2 STICKS TO FORM 2 SQUARES *

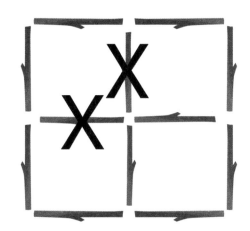

P. 14: NUMBER PUZZLE

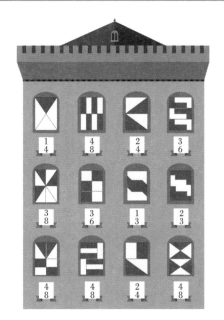

P. 15: THE WINDY TOWER

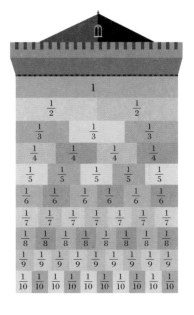

P. 16: WINDOW FRACTIONS

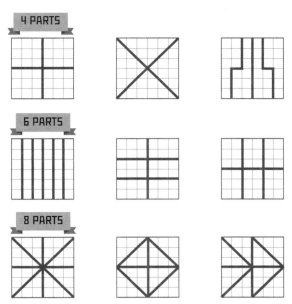

P. 17: DIVIDING GRIDS INTO EQUAL PARTS *

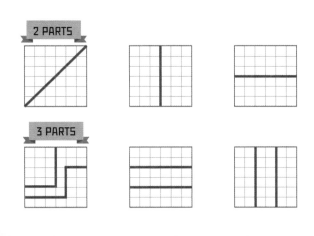

$$\frac{1}{4} > \frac{1}{6} \qquad \mathbf{\frac{5}{6}} > \mathbf{\frac{4}{5}}$$

$$\frac{4}{7} < \frac{2}{3} \qquad 1 > \frac{9}{10}$$

$$\frac{4}{8} = \frac{1}{2} \qquad \frac{2}{6} = \frac{1}{3}$$

$$\frac{1}{9} \quad \frac{2}{10} \quad \frac{1}{3} \quad \frac{3}{7} \quad \frac{2}{4} \quad \frac{6}{8} \quad \frac{6}{7}$$

$$\frac{1}{5} \quad \boxed{\frac{1}{8}}\boxed{\frac{1}{2}} \quad \frac{1}{3} \qquad \boxed{\frac{1}{6}} \quad \frac{4}{6} \quad \frac{3}{6} \quad \boxed{\frac{5}{6}}$$

$$\frac{2}{8} \quad \boxed{\frac{1}{5}} \quad \frac{3}{7} \quad \boxed{\frac{3}{6}}$$

$$\frac{2}{4} \qquad \frac{1}{2} \qquad \frac{3}{6} \qquad \boxed{\frac{2}{5}}$$

$$\frac{2}{6} \qquad \boxed{\frac{7}{8}} \qquad \frac{3}{9} \qquad \frac{1}{3}$$

$$\frac{6}{6} \qquad \boxed{\frac{9}{10}} \qquad \frac{9}{9} \qquad 1$$

$$\frac{4}{7} + \frac{3}{7} = 1 \qquad \frac{5}{10} + \frac{5}{10} = 1$$

$$\frac{1}{4} + \frac{1}{2} + \frac{1}{4} = 1 \qquad \frac{1}{3} + \frac{2}{3} = 1$$

$$\frac{2}{4} + \frac{1}{8} + \frac{3}{8} = 1$$

$$\frac{1}{2} + \frac{1}{2} = 1 \qquad \frac{1}{3} + \frac{1}{3} = \frac{2}{3}$$

$$\frac{1}{2} + \frac{1}{4} = \frac{3}{4} \qquad \frac{2}{3} + \frac{1}{6} = \frac{5}{6}$$

$$\frac{4}{8} + \frac{1}{2} = 1 \qquad \frac{3}{6} + \frac{1}{4} + \frac{2}{8} = 1$$

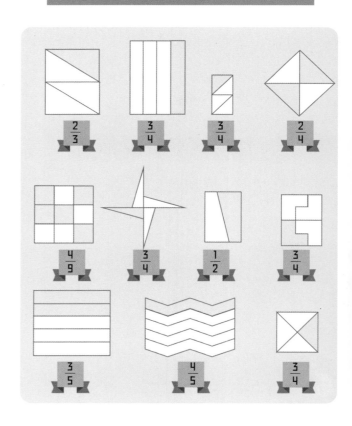

PP. 25: TRICKY TILES

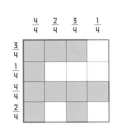

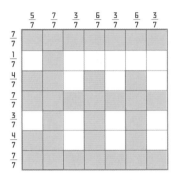

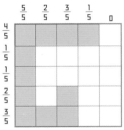

P. 27: COLOR THE FLAMES

PP. 28-29

1) TO FIND OUT HOW THE CIDER WOULD BE POURED EQUALLY INTO THE THREE GLASSES, ADD UP ALL THREE FRACTIONS. $\frac{1}{2} + \frac{1}{4} + \frac{3}{4} = \frac{6}{4}$. IF YOU DIVIDE $\frac{6}{4}$ INTO THREE GLASSES, YOU WOULD POUR $\frac{2}{4}$, $\frac{2}{4}$, AND $\frac{2}{4}$. SO EACH GLASS WOULD BE $\frac{1}{2}$ FULL.

2) THE DRAGON HAS 9 MARBLES UNDER HIS RIGHT PAW AND 16 MARBLES UNDER HIS LEFT PAW.

3) THE DRAGON HAS 4 SQUARES OF CHOCOLATE LEFT TO EAT ON SUNDAY. THIS IS $\frac{1}{8}$ OF THE TOTAL BAR.

4) AFTER EATING 7 CHOCOLATES THE FLAME WOULD BE PUT OUT.

5)

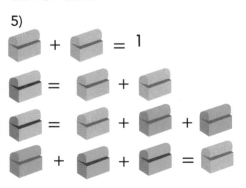

PP. 30-31

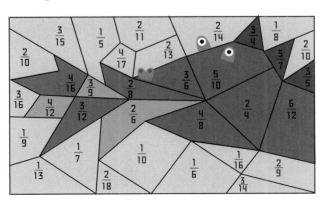

53

P. 33: THE PENGUIN GUARDIANS

"TWO OF US ARE LYING" IS THE ONLY TRUE STATEMENT.
"ONE OF US IS LYING" IS FALSE. IF THE STATEMENT WERE TRUE, THEN TWO PENGUINS WOULD BE TELLING THE TRUTH, WHICH ISN'T POSSIBLE.
"THREE OF US ARE LYING" IS ALSO FALSE. IF THE STATEMENT WERE TRUE, THEN NONE OF THE PENGUINS WOULD BE TELLING THE TRUTH.

P. 34: SCARVES, SOCKS, AND HATS

$\frac{3}{8}$ OF 16=(16÷8)X3=6

$\frac{2}{5}$ OF 15=(15÷5)X2=6

$\frac{3}{7}$ OF 35=(35÷7)X3=15

$\frac{5}{6}$ OF 42=(42÷6)X5=35

$\frac{4}{9}$ OF 81=(81÷9)X4=36

$\frac{2}{8}$ OF 24=(24÷8)X2=6

P. 35: SNOWMEN

1) THERE ARE 25 SNOWMEN TOTAL. IF $\frac{1}{5}$ HAVE RED GLOVES, THEN 5 SNOWMEN HAVE RED GLOVES.
2) THERE ARE 20 SNOWMEN WHO DO NOT HAVE RED GLOVES. $\frac{3}{10}$ OF 20 IS 6.
3) THERE ARE 14 SNOWMEN WITHOUT RED GLOVES OR STRIPED SCARVES. $\frac{4}{7}$ OF 14 IS 8.
4) 8 + 6 + 5 = 19. IF THERE ARE 25 SNOWMEN TOTAL, THEN 6 DO NOT HAVE RED GLOVES, STRIPED SCARVES, OR GREEN HATS.

P. 36: LOCK 1

1) (15 X 2) + 7 = 30
2) (48 ÷ 6) X 4 - 5 = 27
3) (16 ÷ 8) X 5 + (36 ÷ 9) X 7 = 38
4) (25 ÷ 5) X 4 = 20
5) (21 ÷ 7) X 3 X (16 ÷ 8) X 2 = 36
6) (125 ÷ 5) X 2 = 50
7) (56 ÷ 8) X 4 X 4 = 112
8) (18 ÷ 2) + (35 ÷ 7) X 4 = 29

P. 37: LOCK 2

1) (63 ÷ 7)X5=45
2) 56-(56 ÷ 8X5)=56-35=21
3) 54-(54 ÷ 9X7)=54-42=12
4) (5X60) ÷ 4X3=300 ÷ 4X3=225

P. 38-39: FRACTIONS PROBLEMS

1) $\frac{3}{5}$ OF 840 IS 504 RUBIES. 840 TOTAL GEMS - 504 RUBIES = 336 SAPPHIRES
2) $\frac{3}{14}$ OF 840 GEMS = 660. YOU MUST THEN ADD THE 1 DIAMOND HE EXCHANGED TO GET 661.
3) 18 PENGUINS ($\frac{3}{6}$ OR $\frac{1}{2}$ OF 36 = 18). THERE ARE 18 ANIMALS LEFT. 7 SEALS. 11 WALRUSES (7 SEALS + 4)
4) GLACIERS: $\frac{2}{5}$ OF 125 BOOKS = 50 BOOKS
125 BOOKS - 50 BOOKS = 75 BOOKS REMAINING. SNOWSTORMS: $\frac{2}{3}$ OF 75 = 50 BOOKS. IGLOOS: 125 - 50 - 50 = 25 REMAINING BOOKS ABOUT IGLOOS
5) $\frac{3}{4}$ OF 16 = 12 LITERS. IF HE DRINKS $\frac{1}{2}$ A LITER EACH DAY AND HE HAS 12 LITERS TOTAL, HE HAS ENOUGH JUICE TO LAST 24 DAYS.

P. 41: CONNECT THE BRICKS WITH 4 LINES

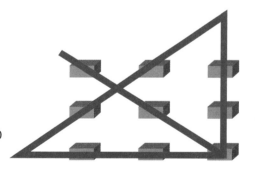

P. 42: OBJECTS UNDER THE GLASS

AMULETS HIDDEN: 2	IN TOTAL: 6
COINS HIDDEN: 16	IN TOTAL: 28
BEETLES HIDDEN: 14	IN TOTAL: 22
PENDANTS HIDDEN: 15	IN TOTAL: 25

P. 43: HIEROGLYPHS

B   C   B   →

1) 30   2) 375   3) 20

1) TOTAL SURFACE AREA OF THE DECORATION: 36 IN²
2) SURFACE AREA OF THE ORANGE PIECES: 10 IN²
3) SURFACE AREA OF THE GREEN PIECES: 5 IN²
4) SURFACE AREA OF THE LIGHT BROWN PIECES: 3 IN²
5) SURFACE AREA OF THE DARK BROWN PIECES: 7 IN²
6) SURFACE AREA OF THE YELLOW PIECES: 11 IN²

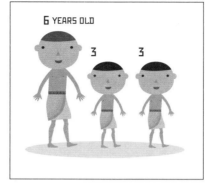

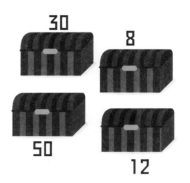

SINCE THE PARCHMENTS WERE DIVIDED INTO FIVE EQUAL GROUPS, THE TOTAL NUMBER IS A MULTIPLE OF 5. POSSIBLE ANSWERS INCLUDE: 10, 15, 20, 25, 30, 35.
THE ONLY NUMBER THAT DIVIDES INTO 4 GROUPS WITH ONE LEFTOVER IS 25.

AT LEAST 5 GOLDEN BEETLES HAVE GEMS ON THEIR BACKS.

PP. 46-47: THE FINAL CHALLENGE

1) THE AGE OF THE MUMMIES: 156, 156, 312

2) THE TANK OF THE CROCODILES: 448, 72, 64

3) THE TOMBS:

4) THE BRICKS: HALF OF ONE BRICK WEIGHS 3 POUNDS, SO A WHOLE BRICK WEIGHS 6 POUNDS. 5 BRICKS WEIGH 30 POUNDS.

5) THE TANGLED BANDAGE: 21 MINUTES

6) MISTER X: 20 SECONDS

Linda Bertola

Graduated in Foreign Languages for Intercultural Mediation at the Università Cattolica di Milano, Linda Bertola is a linguistic and learning aid. She works in education and learning support for students with learning difficulties and special educational needs, both in the scholastic and extra-scholastic ambits. She is also specialized in teaching Italian to foreigners, both children and adults. She has collaborated with schools and associations as an intercultural educator. With her love of education, maths and learning through play, she writes about education on *genitoricrescono.com*. In recent years she has enthusiastically and creatively studied and written a number of volumes for White Star Kids.

Agnese Baruzzi

Born in 1980, she graduated in Graphic Design at ISIA (Higher Institute for Artistic Industries) in Urbino. Since 2001, she has worked as an illustrator and author, working on a number of books for children in Italy, United Kingdom, Japan, Portugal, United States, France and Korea. She holds workshops for children and adults in schools and libraries and collaborates with agencies, graphics studios and publishing houses. In recent years she has enthusiastically and creatively illustrated a number of volumes for White Star Kids.

New York

FLASH KIDS and the distinctive Flash Kids logo are registered trademarks of Barnes and Noble, Inc.

© 2017 White Star s.r.l.

First Flash Kids edition published in 2018.

ISBN 978-1-4114-7909-8

Distributed in Canada by Sterling Publishing c/o Canadian Manda Group, 664 Annette Street Toronto, Ontario, M6S 2C8, Canada

For information about custom editions, special sales, and premium and corporate purchases, please contact Sterling Special Sales at 800-805-5489 or specialsales@ sterlingpublishing.com.

Manufactured in China
Lot #:
2 4 6 8 10 9 7 5 3 1
01/18

flashkids.com

Translation: Iceigeo, Milan (translator: Emma Jane Williams, Simone Gramegna)

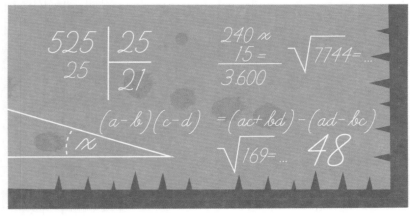

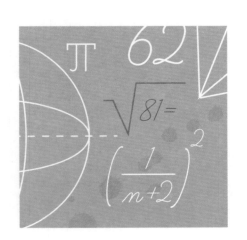

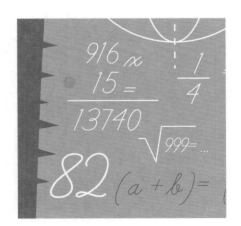

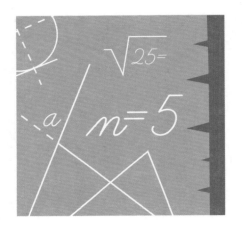

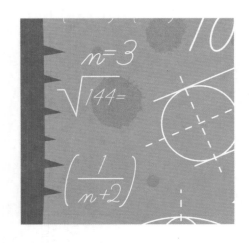

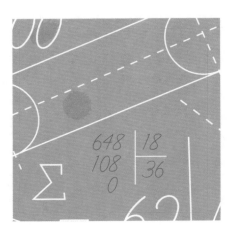

THESE STICKERS ARE PIECES OF THE TABLET. EACH TIME YOU EARN ONE, PLACE IT ONE PAGE 48.

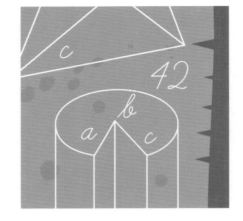

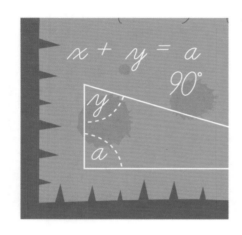

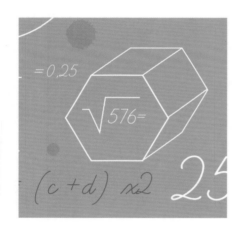

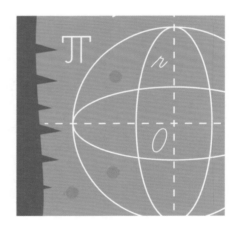

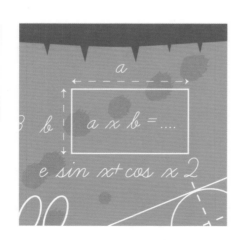

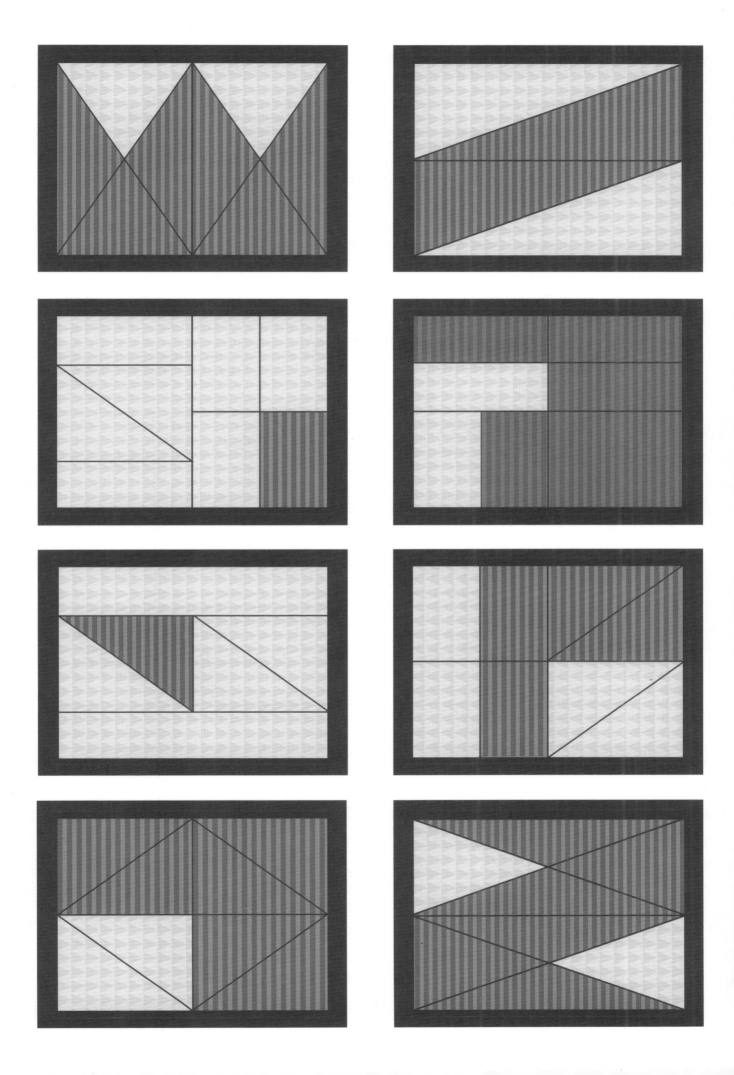

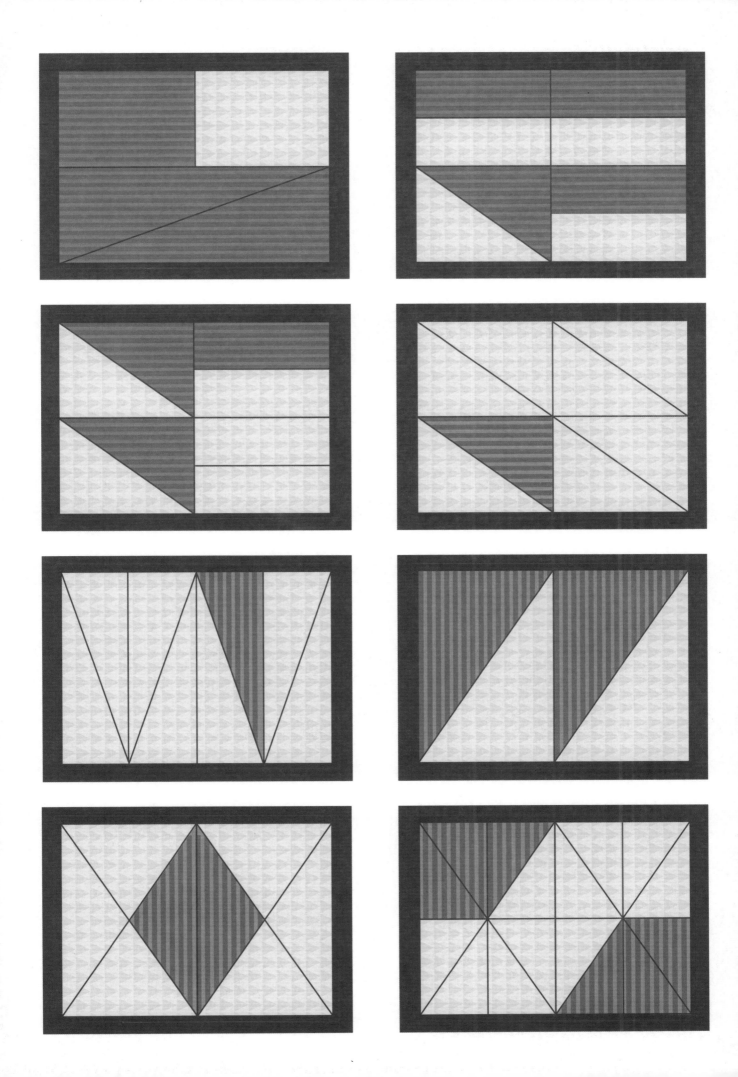

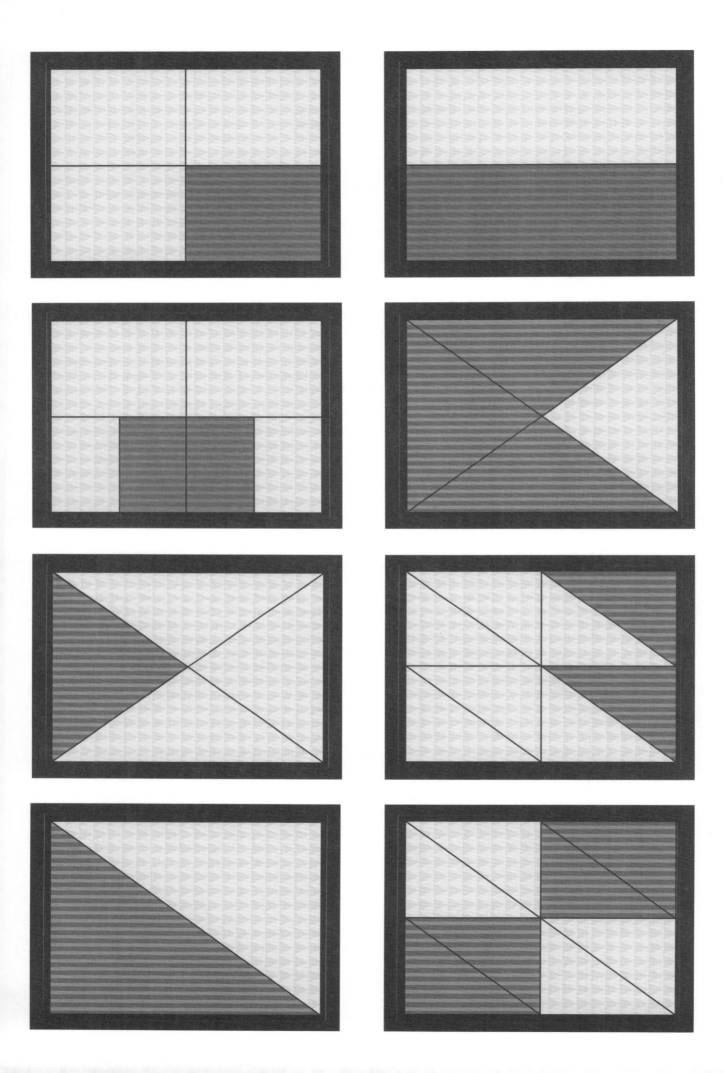

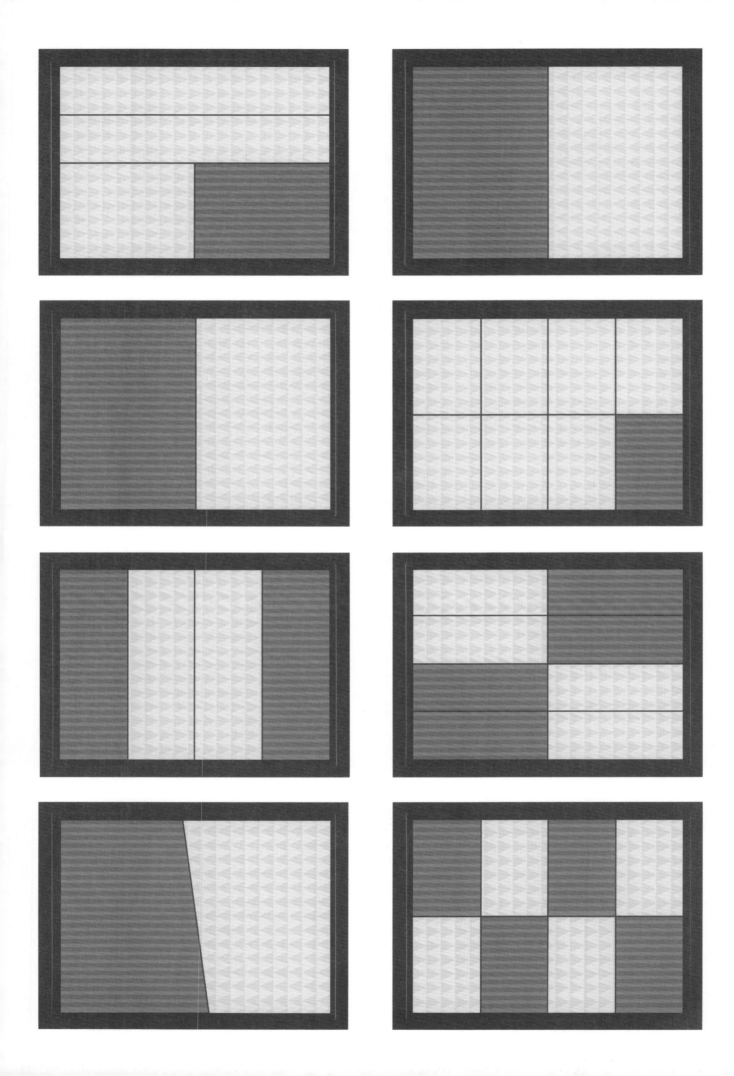

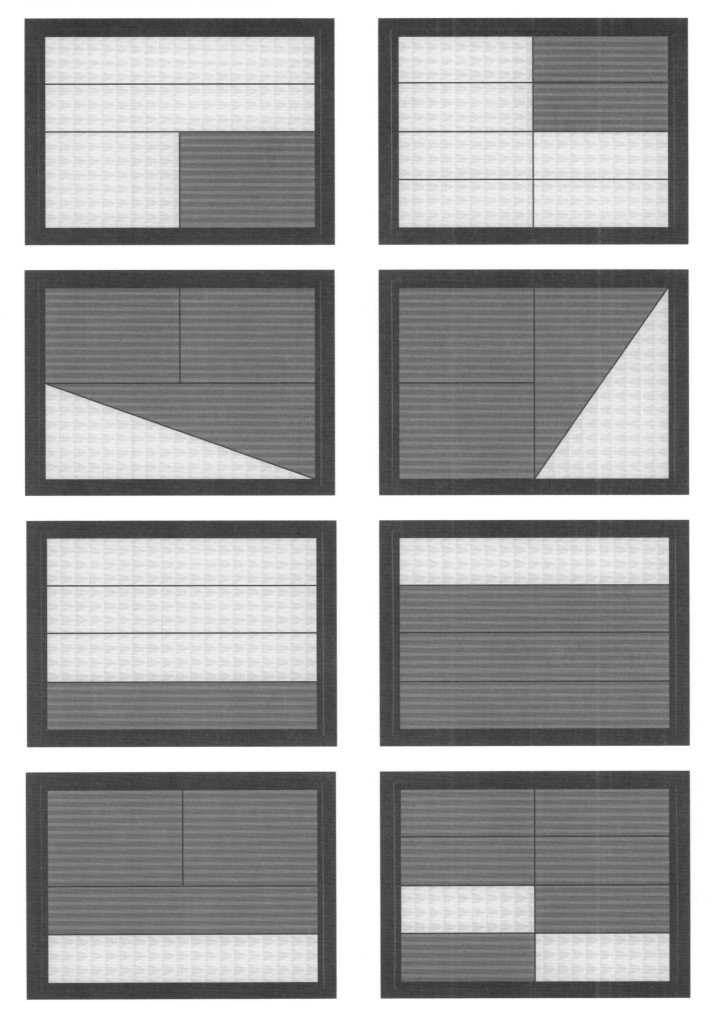

1									

| $\dfrac{1}{2}$ | | | | | $\dfrac{1}{2}$ | | | | |

| $\dfrac{1}{3}$ | | | $\dfrac{1}{3}$ | | | $\dfrac{1}{3}$ | | | |

| $\dfrac{1}{4}$ | | $\dfrac{1}{4}$ | | $\dfrac{1}{4}$ | | $\dfrac{1}{4}$ | | | |

| $\dfrac{1}{5}$ | $\dfrac{1}{5}$ | | $\dfrac{1}{5}$ | $\dfrac{1}{5}$ | | $\dfrac{1}{5}$ | | | |

| $\dfrac{1}{6}$ | $\dfrac{1}{6}$ | $\dfrac{1}{6}$ | $\dfrac{1}{6}$ | $\dfrac{1}{6}$ | $\dfrac{1}{6}$ | | | | |

| $\dfrac{1}{7}$ | $\dfrac{1}{7}$ | $\dfrac{1}{7}$ | $\dfrac{1}{7}$ | $\dfrac{1}{7}$ | $\dfrac{1}{7}$ | $\dfrac{1}{7}$ | | | |

| $\dfrac{1}{8}$ | $\dfrac{1}{8}$ | $\dfrac{1}{8}$ | $\dfrac{1}{8}$ | $\dfrac{1}{8}$ | $\dfrac{1}{8}$ | $\dfrac{1}{8}$ | $\dfrac{1}{8}$ | | |

| $\dfrac{1}{9}$ | $\dfrac{1}{9}$ | $\dfrac{1}{9}$ | $\dfrac{1}{9}$ | $\dfrac{1}{9}$ | $\dfrac{1}{9}$ | $\dfrac{1}{9}$ | $\dfrac{1}{9}$ | $\dfrac{1}{9}$ | |

| $\dfrac{1}{10}$ | $\dfrac{1}{10}$ | $\dfrac{1}{10}$ | $\dfrac{1}{10}$ | $\dfrac{1}{10}$ | $\dfrac{1}{10}$ | $\dfrac{1}{10}$ | $\dfrac{1}{10}$ | $\dfrac{1}{10}$ | $\dfrac{1}{10}$ |